The Instant Pot®
No-Pressure Cookbook

THE INSTANT POT®
No-Pressure Cookbook

100 Low-Stress,
High-Flavor Recipes

Laurel Randolph
Photographs by Staci Valentine

ST. MARTIN'S GRIFFIN
NEW YORK

THE INSTANT POT® NO-PRESSURE COOKBOOK.
Copyright © 2018 by Laurel Randolph. All rights reserved. Printed in the United States of America. For information, address St. Martin's Press, 175 Fifth Avenue, New York, N.Y. 10010.

www.stmartins.com

Photographs by Staci Valentine
Book design by Richard Oriolo

The Library of Congress Cataloging-in-Publication Data is available upon request.

ISBN 978-1-250-18558-7 (trade paperback)
ISBN 978-1-250-18559-4 (ebook)

Our books may be purchased in bulk for promotional, educational, or business use. Please contact your local bookseller or the Macmillan Corporate and Premium Sales Department at 1-800-221-7945, extension 5442, or by email at MacmillanSpecialMarkets@macmillan.com.

FIRST EDITION: May 2018

10 9 8 7 6 5 4 3 2 1

Endless thanks to a fantastic group of ladies for all of their help:
Sara, Keri, Vicki, and Lillian

CONTENTS

Introduction

B'Fast

Meaty Mains

Veggie Mains

Veggie Sides

Grainy and Beany Sides

Soups and Stews

Sauces and Sweet Stuff

The Instant Pot®
No-Pressure Cookbook

INTRODUCTION

Do you love to cook? Do you love pressure cooking? How about food, do you like food? A lot? Then keep reading, because this is the book for you.

So you own an Instant Pot and you've made some things with it. You like the convenience of the cooker, but you're still figuring out how to get the most out of the device. And you're getting a little tired of making lots and lots of soups. I hear you! It's time to think outside of the Instant Pot—it's not just for one-pot meals or combining prepackaged ingredients. You can make flavorful, lively dishes using fresh ingredients. Your pressure cooker can be as essential to your kitchen as your coffee maker or your microwave. Don't just pull out your cooker every once in a while. Give it a place of honor on your kitchen counter.

There are lots of reasons to love pressure cooking—speed, convenience, nutrition, flavor. That's why I'm pumped that this cooking method is having a real comeback. New electric pressure cookers and multi-cookers like the Instant Pot make pressure cooking easy and practical, and they're flying off the shelves. Gone are the days of constantly monitoring a stovetop cooker and praying that it doesn't literally blow up in your face. Electric versions are super safe and automated, allowing you to set it and walk away. But don't walk away for too long because it's fast, okay?

Too many people approach the electric pressure cooker the same way they would a slow cooker. Dump in a few ingredients and some-odd minutes later you have a meal of meat and starch. There's nothing wrong with this method, but it pushes the pressure cooker into a slow cooker–esque corner. And no one puts the pressure cooker in a corner. It's time we look beyond one-pot dump meals and an obsession with fast cook times and view this electric wonder as a key component of a twenty-first-century kitchen.

Use your Instant Pot to make a side dish, freeing up your stovetop for frying and your oven for roasting. Make your breakfast while you shower, or make dessert while you make dinner. An electric pressure cooker can help you put together a gourmet dinner on a Tuesday night, churning out al pastor in no time at all. It can produce big flavors and fun dishes, not just pot roast (no offense, pot roast). And did I mention that it doesn't heat up your home, making it pretty darn energy efficient?

This cookbook is not an instruction manual. You probably got one of those with your Instant Pot. If you're new to pressure cooking, be sure to give your manual a thorough reading and perform a few test runs making plain rice or beans to get a feel for the functionality.

But even if you've studied your manual cover to cover and played with your cooker a lot, I've still got a few pro tips coming up. After making dish after dish with an Instant Pot, I've learned a thing or two and now I want to pass that hard-won knowledge on to you.

Finally, thank you for buying this book. I hope you enjoy reading it and using it—that's kind of the point. Cooking should be fun, and cooking with pressure is no exception. So have fun!

The Real Reasons Why
Pressure Cooking Is Great

First things first, I'd like to talk about the real-life yays and nays of using a pressure cooker as part of your kitchen arsenal and dispel a few myths.

YAY! Ease of use. The Instant Pot is admittedly a little weird when you first get acquainted. It beeps at you, there's a lot of buttons, and it has a big, heavy lid. But once you learn what buttons to push and can remember to close the valve, the cooker does everything else and you can sit back and relax.

NAY. There's not a lot of room for random improvisation. For most dishes, they need to cook for a fairly specific amount of time to avoid under- or overcooking them, and if you add too little liquid then you're screwed. You can't just throw random things in and adjust as you go like you can on the stovetop. But as you progress in your pressure cooking journey, you'll learn what does and doesn't work and come up with plenty of your own signature dishes.

YAY! Flavor. In most circumstances, the pressure cooker is great for locking in flavor. It cooks food in less time without aggressive boiling and with less liquid. This means more flavor for your mouth.

NAY. You can't cook everything. Some things are just plain bad under pressure: really delicate items or anything you want to be crispy or roasty. Most baked goods. I could go on, but I think you get the picture. The general rule (that sometimes gets broken) is to only pressure cook foods that normally get boiled, braised, stewed, or steamed. Delicate items are typically added after the pressure cooking is over. There are a few surprises, but stop trying to make everything in there.

YAY! Time. An Instant Pot can greatly cut down on cooking time, especially for big hunks of tough meat and dried beans, which take half the time of traditional methods.

NAY. Not everything takes less time. Remember that the cooker takes time to heat up, cook, and then release pressure. That being said, there are plenty of reasons to use your Instant Pot other than simply saving a few minutes (see above!), and with the help of this book, you're guaranteed to get the most out of your treasured appliance.

A Note on Instant Pot Models

All of the recipes in this book will work with all Instant Pot models and sizes, including the Ultra. Note that the reimagined pressure release valve on the Ultra makes it safer and easier to release steam, but it takes longer to do so whether using a quick or natural release. The model really holds pressure well, and in my experience it can take twice as long to release pressure naturally as opposed to older models. If you're like me, you get impatient and want to eat now now now. As a general rule, if it's been 30 minutes and the pressure has not fully released from your Ultra, use a controlled quick release to release the remaining pressure.

Things That I Forget to Do Sometimes and You Might Forget Too

- Double-check that the sealing ring/gasket is properly in place under the lid.

- Make sure you have enough liquid for the cooker to come up to pressure. The minimum amount of liquid is typically 1 cup, but can differ depending on how thick your liquid is or what you're cooking.

- Don't overfill! Especially if you're cooking grains, beans, or rice. Halfway is the safe point for dishes that grow in size and produce foam.

- When locking the lid, double check that it is fully locked and sealed by gently lifting the cooker by the handle straight up from the counter.

- Close the vent! If you're not using a fancy new model of the Instant Pot, you need to manually close the vent before cooking. This one's easy to forget.

- Use a towel to protect your hand when performing a quick release and step away from the steam.

Equipment

Don't freak out! This cookbook doesn't use lots of special equipment beyond your electric pressure cooker, but there are a few items beyond bowls and spoons that will be useful to you:

TRIVET

The Instant Pot comes with a metal trivet that sits perfectly in the bottom of the cooker pot. Keep it! It comes in handy in a number of recipes. Alternatively, an appropriately sized steamer basket with legs will usually work. Which leads me to...

STEAMER BASKET

Even though only a couple of recipes in this book require a steamer basket, the Instant Pot is great for steaming all sorts of foods. You'll want a metal basket with legs and a center ring for easy removal that fits inside your cooker.

MUGS/RAMEKINS

Most of the recipes in this book cook directly in the pot of the cooker, but a couple utilize mugs or ramekins to keep food from scorching. Regular old coffee mugs work just fine, or you can use baking ramekins that hold the same volume—just double check that they fit in your cooker! Make sure that whatever containers you use are heatproof ceramic or tempered glass or you'll have a real mess on your hands.

BAKING PAN

Does Salted Caramel Flan sound good to you? Then you'll need a 7- or 8-inch baking pan that fits inside your Instant Pot. Even though only one recipe in this book requires such a pan, it's great for making pressure cooker cheesecakes and quiches, too.

EXTRA RINGS

This isn't required, but I highly recommend owning at least two sealing rings/silicone gaskets (that's the removable rubbery ring inside the lid). These rings tend to soak up smells, so I have one for smelly chilis and curries and one for oatmeal and other less smelly things. Plus, they're cheap, readily available online, and handy to have as a backup.

Terminology

You'll notice that a few terms and phrases come up over and over again when reading a pressure cooker recipe. For quick reference, here's what the heck I'm talking about when I use the following terminology:

SAUTÉ FUNCTION

The Sauté function allows you to sauté right inside the Instant Pot. The recipes in this book use the function to soften, brown, and simmer at various stages in the recipe, improving flavor and texture. It must be used with the lid unlocked, and can be adjusted to low, medium, or high. Unless otherwise noted as high or low, the recipes in this book use the medium Sauté setting. This is the default Sauté temperature on the Instant Pot, which means when you press Sauté it automatically preheats to medium. To turn off the Sauté function, press the Cancel button.

HIGH PRESSURE/LOW PRESSURE

When using your Instant Pot to pressure cook (and every recipe in this cookbook does just that), you can adjust the setting to low or high pressure. Low pressure is good for delicate foods like eggs, while high pressure is much more common and is used for the majority of pressure cooking recipes. The pressure level is specified for every recipe in this book.

NATURAL RELEASE

There are two major ways to release pressure once your cook time has elapsed. A natural release means the pressure slowly releases on its own from the cooker. This can take anywhere from a few minutes to half an hour, depending on how high you filled your pot and how long it was under pressure. It's the preferred method for many recipes, since the dish continues to slowly cook under the decreasing pressure, and allows any foam to die down. Some recipes use a natural release for 5 to 20 minutes followed by a quick release.

QUICK RELEASE

The other major option for releasing pressure is a quick release. This requires you to open the vent once the cook time has elapsed and manually release the steam. Be careful not to leave your hand, face, or any other body part over the vent, and position the cooker so that the steam is not released directly onto cabinets or walls (unless you want your paint stripped, in which case blast those cabinets!). This release is used to save time and to avoid overcooking, but is not recommended for all recipes.

CONTROLLED QUICK RELEASE

This book, on occasion, uses a controlled quick release. This is a slower, less aggressive way of releasing the steam than a normal quick release, and can help avoid splatters. For some Instant Pot models, this can be done by gently pushing the knob toward the venting position without shifting it all the way over, and holding it there. For the Ultra, the release button can be pressed lightly to gradually release steam without locking it into place. Keep a kitchen towel handy when using a controlled quick release, and be careful not to scald your hand.

A NOTE ABOUT THE CANCEL BUTTON

All recipes in this book are written assuming that the Keep Warm function will not be used. Many Instant Pot models automatically turn on the Keep Warm function once the cook time has ended. You can turn off this function (and you should) by pressing the Cancel button. New Instant Pot models allow you to turn off the Keep Warm function before you even begin. This is especially important for some recipes, such as any involving polenta, where the Keep Warm function can cause scorching.

Ingredients Worth Mentioning

You may notice that this cookbook has more fun ingredients than your standard pressure cooker cookbook. I love cooking with all kinds of fresh produce and interesting spices, but I tried to only include items that most people can find in their local market (if you're living at a research station in Antarctica, I can't help you [but also, wow!]). A few ingredients might be hard to find for those of you living in a bit of a food desert, but everything can be ordered online nowadays. I also suggest planning to make certain recipes after a trip to a nearby food-rich town.

While I'm here, I'd like to encourage everyone to visit your local international markets that specialize in foods from specific countries and regions. Not only do they have the best selection and often the best prices, you'll encounter all sorts of items you don't normally find in your standard grocery and it's all super tasty. And since this book calls for lots of fresh fruit and veg, visit a farmers' market if it is available to you. There's no better place to get produce than directly from the farmer's hands.

Here are some notes on specific ingredients that pop up throughout the book and need a little background info:

BROTH

Many, many recipes in this book call for vegetable, chicken, or beef broth as the principal liquid. I highly recommend that you make your own broth. I don't just recommend it, I triple dog dare ya. I toss all of my veggie scraps and chicken bones in a freezer bag, and once the bag is full, it's time to brew up some broth. It's incredibly easy to make in the Instant Pot anyway, so no excuses. Here are some general guidelines when making broth:

MUSTS Onions, carrots, celery, bay leaf (any of these can be scraps except the bay leaf).

OPTIONALS Chicken bones/leftover meat (if you're making chicken broth), mushrooms, scallions, shallots, garlic, tomatoes, peas, parsnips, turnips, broccoli, cabbage, spinach, chard, parsley, corn.

HOW TO Add the scraps, veggies, and/or bones to your Instant Pot. Add enough water to cover (but don't overfill). Cook on high pressure for 1 hour and use a natural release. Strain well and store in the fridge for up to 5 days or the freezer for a month.

BEANS

One thing a pressure cooker is great at is cooking dried beans. It cuts the time down considerably and makes it a hands-off task. Note that the cook time for beans can vary depending on how old the beans are, so always taste your beans after cooking to see if they need a little more time. Here are some notes on cooking dried beans, which I call for frequently in this book:

PREP Always rinse your beans and pick through them to find and discard any bad beans (shriveled, really discolored) or rocks (yes, I have found a pebble or two). Drain well.

PRESOAKING Some of my recipes call for presoaked beans and some of them don't. Presoaking cuts down the cook time and helps keep the beans more intact when cooking. Some argue that it also makes them more digestible, cutting down on bean-related gas. But who knows! Either way, here's how to presoak your beans:

After rinsing and picking over your dried beans, place them in a bowl and cover them with a few inches of cold water. Let them sit overnight, or for at least 6 hours and no more than 24. If your house or apartment is warmer than normal room temperature, stash them in the fridge. Drain.

If you forgot to do that (whoops), you can quick soak your beans. They won't be quite as pretty, but they'll work just fine. Add the beans to your Instant Pot and add enough water to cover them by a few inches. Turn on the Sauté function and bring the water to a boil. Turn off the Sauté function and secure the lid. Cook at high pressure for 2 minutes and use a quick release. Drain.

TOMATOES AND OTHER ACIDIC FOODS

When cooking beans from dried, adding raw tomato or other highly acidic foods can inhibit cooking and make the beans tough. It's best to add acidic ingredients like tomatoes, vinegar, and citrus after cooking.

GARLIC

If you've flipped through this book, you may think I reeeeally like garlic. I do love garlic (screw you, vampires), but I also call for more than the usual amount because pressure cooking can often dull the taste. I make up for this by adding extra and by sometimes adding whole, smashed cloves instead of minced garlic.

WINE

I love cooking with wine, but when you add the boozy stuff, make sure to cook most of the alcohol off before pressure cooking. Since no steam escapes when under pressure, the alcohol can stay in the food rather than just leaving behind its nice flavor. That's why all of the recipes using wine in this recipe simmer before pressure cooking.

A Note on No-No Foods

While reading your manual and researching your pressure cooker, you may have noticed that some foods are not recommended for pressure cooking, such as pasta, barley, and oatmeal. You may have also noticed that I include many of these restricted ingredients in my recipes. I have pressure cooked with these foods time and time again without incident, and you will too. The key is to take a few precautions when cooking them:

- Fill the pot less than half full and give the ingredients space to foam up without clogging the vent. Don't double or triple the recipes featuring these ingredients willy-nilly. Make sure you have plenty of room in your cooker.

- Add a dose of oil. I include oil in recipes featuring these ingredients, but make sure you don't leave it out. Oil helps keep foaming to a minimum.

- Use a natural release. Since these foods can foam up so much, using a natural release for at least part of the pressure releasing process is important. A quick release could cause hot liquid to spray out of the valve and that's no fun for anyone.

  NOTE: If the no-no ingredient is added after pressure cooking, then don't sweat! Proceed as usual, since foaming won't be an issue.

Adjusting Recipes

Many recipes in this cookbook can be halved, doubled, or altered in other ways but some cannot. Here are some questions to ask yourself before you start experimenting:

WILL THE RECIPE HAVE LESS THAN I CUP OF LIQUID IN IT? You cannot halve a recipe that won't leave enough liquid for the cooker to come to pressure. The standard amount of liquid needed is 1 cup, but can be less if the items you're cooking will immediately release lots of water, or can be more if the liquid is thick (like tomato sauce).

WILL IT FILL THE COOKER OVER HALF FULL? Depending on what you're cooking, you don't want to fill the cooker over halfway, especially if you're not using a natural release. Filling the cooker too much, particularly if any of the items are known to foam and bubble up, can lead to a clogged valve or splatters of hot liquid all over your pretty kitchen.

WILL I NEED TO ADJUST THE COOK TIME? If you're simply doubling a soup or a dish with pieces of meat or veggies, then the cook time will remain the same. If you're doubling a recipe with a piece of meat and replacing it with a giant piece of meat, you will need to adjust your cook time so that the meat cooks all the way through. When adjusting the size of items in a recipe, do some research before assuming a cook time.

B'fast

Savory Chickpeas and Tomatoes with Fried Eggs

Spiced Farro with Stewed Plums

Breakfast Sausage and Corn Congee

Spiced Banana Steel-Cut Oats for Two

Steamed Egg Cups

Breakfast Deviled Eggs

Brown Rice Breakfast Risotto

Shakshuka with Harissa and Feta

Cherry and Chocolate Chip Oatmeal

Brown Butter and Pear Wheat Berry Bowl

Polenta and Soft-Boiled Eggs with Gremolata

Savory Chickpeas and Tomatoes with Fried Eggs

If you don't include beans in your breakfast rotation, maybe this tomato and chickpea dish will change your mind. Chickpeas, also known as garbanzo beans, turn creamy but not mushy after stewing in tomatoes and garlic. The tomatoes aren't added until the end since they can inhibit cooking and make beans tough. Top each serving with one or two fried eggs (depending on your appetite) for a satisfying way to start the day. SERVES 3

1 cup dried chickpeas, presoaked and drained (see page 9)

2 teaspoons olive oil

1 bay leaf

4 cups water

2 garlic cloves, minced

1 (14.5-ounce) can diced tomatoes, with juice

Salt and pepper

2 tablespoons sour cream

1 tablespoon canola or grapeseed oil

3 to 6 large eggs

1 tablespoon chopped fresh parsley

COMBINE presoaked chickpeas, 1 teaspoon olive oil, the bay leaf, and water in your Instant Pot. Secure the lid.

COOK at high pressure for 12 minutes and use a natural release.

ONCE the pressure has released, drain the beans and remove the bay leaf. Wipe out the pot and return it to the cooker. Turn on the Sauté function on low.

ONCE hot, add the remaining 1 teaspoon olive oil. Add the garlic and sauté for 30 seconds. Add the drained chickpeas and the tomatoes with juice. Season with salt and pepper. Loosely place the lid on top with the vent open and simmer for about 10 minutes, until the chickpeas have reached the desired tenderness. Turn off the Sauté function. Add the sour cream and taste for seasoning.

HEAT a large skillet over medium heat. Once hot, add the canola oil and coat the pan. Add the eggs, one at a time, spaced evenly apart. Cook, covering with a lid or sheet pan halfway through, until the yolks still jiggle but the whites are mostly firm and the bottom is crispy (3 to 5 minutes). Season with salt and pepper.

SERVE the chickpeas topped with fried eggs and fresh parsley.

P.S. This dish goes well with crusty, warm bread or pita, but leave it out if you're gluten-free.

Spiced Farro with Stewed Plums

Chewy, nutty farro makes a surprisingly good breakfast, whether it's paired with sweet things like fruit and yogurt, or with savory items like eggs and wilted greens. Spiced Farro with Stewed Plums is a wholesome dish that's buttery, lightly sweet, and bursting with spice and juicy plum. And since the fruit cooks with the farro, it's quick and easy, too (I can't handle anything complicated first thing in the morning).

SERVES 3 OR 4

1 tablespoon butter	1 pinch salt
1 cup semi-pearled farro	1½ cups water
1 teaspoon ground cinnamon	2 ripe dark plums, roughly chopped, plus 1 ripe plum, diced
½ teaspoon ground ginger	
1 pinch grated nutmeg	3 tablespoons brown sugar

TURN on the Sauté function. Once hot, add the butter followed by the farro. Sauté for 2 minutes. Turn off the Sauté function.

ADD the cinnamon, ginger, nutmeg, and salt. Stir well. Add the water and 2 roughly chopped plums. Secure the lid.

COOK at high pressure for 10 minutes and use a natural release.

DON'T drain the farro. Add the brown sugar and turn on the Sauté function. Simmer for about 3 minutes or until thickened a bit, stirring to prevent scorching. Let cool for at least 5 minutes to let thicken some more.

SERVE topped with diced fresh plum.

Breakfast Sausage and Corn Congee

Congee is a traditional Asian dish of creamy, stewed rice that's often eaten for breakfast. A typical version includes chicken and maybe some scallions on top, but countless variations exist. My take on the cozy and comforting rice porridge includes crumbled sausage and fresh corn for sweetness and crunch. I highly recommend topping the congee with a poached egg for a bit of richness.

SERVES 4

1 teaspoon canola or grapeseed oil

8 ounces uncooked breakfast sausage, without casing

⅔ cup jasmine or long-grain white rice, rinsed and drained

2½ cups chicken or vegetable broth

2 cups water

Salt and pepper

1 cup fresh corn kernels

1 tablespoon soy sauce

1 teaspoon sesame oil

¼ cup chopped scallions

4 poached, fried, or soft-boiled eggs (optional)

TURN on the Sauté function. Once hot, add the oil followed by the sausage. Cook the sausage, breaking it into small pieces, until no longer pink. Turn off the Sauté function.

ADD the rice, broth, and water. Season with salt and pepper and secure the lid.

COOK at high pressure for 30 minutes and use a natural release.

REMOVE the lid and turn on the Sauté function. Stir. Once bubbling, add the corn, soy sauce, and sesame oil. Cook for 3 minutes, stirring frequently to prevent scorching on the bottom. Turn off the Sauté function.

LET cool for a few minutes and taste for seasoning. It will continue to thicken as it cools. Serve topped with scallions and eggs (if using).

Spiced Banana Steel-Cut Oats for Two

There's no special equipment needed for an adorable, personal-sized breakfast—two regular old heatproof mugs will do ya. Cooking the oatmeal in mugs prevents the milk from scorching, and it makes cleanup for the spiced sweet dish beyond easy. Make sure to use a natural release or you'll have a mess on your hands and you can't blame me! SERVES 2

2½ cups water

½ cup steel-cut oats

1 tablespoon brown sugar

1 teaspoon ground cinnamon

¼ teaspoon ground ginger

⅛ teaspoon ground allspice

⅛ teaspoon salt

1 small very ripe banana, peeled and mashed

⅓ cup milk or nondairy milk (soy, almond, or coconut)

2 teaspoons butter

Toasted walnuts, for serving (optional)

Banana chips, for serving (optional)

ADD 1½ cups water and a trivet to your Instant Pot.

IN a small bowl, mix together the oats, brown sugar, cinnamon, ginger, allspice, and salt. Add equal amounts to two heatproof mugs. Top each with half of the mashed banana. Add ½ cup water and half of the milk to each mug. Carefully stir and top each with 1 teaspoon butter. Place the mugs on the trivet and secure the lid.

COOK at high pressure for 20 minutes and use a natural release.

REMOVE the lid, careful not to drip any condensation onto the mugs. Carefully remove the mugs (they're hot!) and stir. Let sit for 5 to 10 minutes—they will thicken as they cool. Serve topped with toasted walnuts and/or banana chips (if using).

P.S. If you're making oatmeal for one, halve this recipe but use the same amount of water in the bottom of the pot and the same cook time. You can even cook it in a cereal bowl as long as it's heatproof.

Steamed Egg Cups

I have a favorite Korean barbecue restaurant, but it has nothing to do with the barbecue and everything to do with the steamed egg they bring you before every meal. It's hot and savory while being light and fluffy, and I love it. The pressure cooker version is an easy breakfast—just plop each mug on a plate next to some hashbrowns and fruit and you have a meal.   SERVES 2

Cooking spray

3 large eggs

½ cup chicken or vegetable broth

Salt

White pepper (optional)

1 cup water

1 scallion, thinly sliced (optional)

GREASE two heatproof mugs with cooking spray.

IN a small mixing bowl, combine the eggs, broth, a healthy pinch of salt, and a pinch of white pepper (if using). Whisk well until the mixture is completely combined.

STRAIN the mixture equally into the two mugs. Add the water to the Instant Pot and add the trivet. Place the mugs on the trivet and secure the lid.

COOK at low pressure for 5 minutes and use a natural release.

Remove the lid, careful not to drip any condensation onto the mugs. Carefully remove the mugs (they're hot!) and let cool for at least 5 minutes. Serve topped with scallions (if using).

P.S. For extra flavor, top with a sprinkle of cheese or a drizzle of soy sauce.

Breakfast Deviled Eggs

Hosting a brunch? Let me present Breakfast Deviled Eggs: an adorable and crowd-pleasing way to serve eggs that can be made before everyone arrives. The usual mayo is swapped out for breakfasty and healthy yogurt, and a little chopped bacon takes it over the top. If you have more than a few people eating, this recipe is easily doubled. SERVES 4 TO 6

1 cup water

6 large eggs

2 strips bacon, not thick-cut

¼ cup plain yogurt, Greek or regular

¼ teaspoon Dijon mustard

¼ to ½ teaspoon smoked paprika

Salt and pepper

2 teaspoons milk (only if you're using Greek yogurt)

1 teaspoon finely chopped fresh chives, for garnish (optional)

ADD the water and a steamer basket or trivet to your Instant Pot. Place the eggs in the steamer basket or on the trivet (not touching the sides). Secure the lid.

COOK at low pressure for 8 minutes and use a quick release.

MEANWHILE, cook the bacon in a large skillet until crisp. Drain, let cool, and finely chop.

ONCE the pressure has released, place the eggs in an ice water bath. Once cool, tap each egg to gently break the shell and peel. Slice in half from top to bottom and use your hands to gently squeeze out and grab the yolk. Add the yolk to a medium mixing bowl. Repeat with all of the eggs, discarding one of the yolks.

ADD the yogurt, mustard, and paprika (¼ teaspoon for mild deviled eggs, ½ for a little kick) and season with salt and pepper. Mash well until very creamy. If using thick Greek yogurt, add 1 to 2 teaspoons milk to thin. The texture of the mixture should be creamy without being crumbly or runny. Taste for seasoning.

MIX in half of the chopped bacon. Add the mixture to a zip-top bag, squeeze out the excess air, and close the top. Cut a ½-inch hole in a bottom corner of the bag.

PIPE the mixture into each egg white, overfilling slightly. Serve topped with the remaining bacon and chives (if using).

P.S. If you're making these a few hours ahead of time, store in the refrigerator and add the bacon on top just before serving so that it stays crisp.

Brown Rice Breakfast Risotto

Brown Rice Breakfast Risotto is my new favorite breakfast. It's super savory and feels really special, but it's ultimately a no sweat meal-in-a-bowl. The Instant Pot makes perfect soft-boiled eggs in a snap, and while they cool and you cook the bacon, the risotto cooks in the pot. A little cheese and wilted greens completes this unique and comforting morning dish. SERVES 2

I cup water	2¼ cups chicken or vegetable broth
2 large eggs	Salt and pepper
2 tablespoons butter	2 strips bacon
½ medium onion, diced	2 cups loosely packed baby spinach or arugula
2 garlic cloves, minced	
I cup long-grain brown rice	½ cup shredded cheddar, Monterey Jack, or other melty cheese

ADD the water and a steamer basket or trivet to your Instant Pot. Place the eggs in the basket or on the trivet (not touching the sides). Secure the lid.

COOK at low pressure for 4 minutes and use a quick release. Carefully place the eggs in an ice water bath to cool.

REMOVE the steamer basket or trivet, empty the pot, and wipe it out. Turn on the Sauté function. Once hot, add the butter followed by the onion. Sauté for 2 minutes. Add the garlic and rice and sauté for 1 minute. Turn off the Sauté function. Add the broth and season with salt and pepper. Secure the lid.

COOK at high pressure for 23 minutes and use a natural release.

MEANWHILE, cook the bacon until crisp in a large skillet. Let drain and cool slightly, then chop. Carefully peel the eggs, making sure not to pierce the yolks.

ONCE the pressure has released, stir the rice well to achieve a creamy texture. Add the greens, cheese, and half of the bacon and stir to wilt the greens and melt the cheese. Taste for seasoning.

SERVE topped with the remaining bacon and the soft-boiled eggs, cut in half.

Shakshuka with Harissa and Feta

Shakshuka, an egg and tomato sauce dish, and harissa, a flavorful pepper paste, both have North African origins. They also taste great together. Eggs cook right on top of this pleasantly spiced sauce before being topped with feta cheese. Serve with warm pita for breakfast and add a salad for dinner.

SERVES 2 TO 4

2 tablespoons olive oil

½ red bell pepper, finely diced

4 garlic cloves, minced

1 tablespoon harissa paste

1 bay leaf

1 (28-ounce) can diced tomatoes with juice

Salt and pepper

4 large eggs

⅓ cup crumbled feta cheese

2 tablespoons chopped fresh parsley (optional)

TURN on the Sauté function. Once hot, add the oil followed by the bell pepper and garlic. Sauté for 1 minute and add the harissa paste. Stir and turn off the Sauté function. Add the bay leaf and tomatoes with juice. Stir and season with salt and pepper. Secure the lid.

COOK at high pressure for 8 minutes and use a natural release for 5 minutes followed by a quick release.

TURN on the Sauté function. Simmer, uncovered, for 5 minutes, stirring occasionally. Crack the eggs, one at a time, into a small bowl. Lower each one into the pot to cook in the sauce, spacing them out and avoiding the edges of the pot. Cook for 2 minutes uncovered, then loosely cover and cook until the whites are mostly set but the yolks are still runny, 1 to 2 minutes (3 to 4 minutes total).

TURN off the Sauté function. To keep the eggs from overcooking, promptly remove the pot from the Instant Pot and sprinkle with the feta followed by parsley (if using). Serve.

Cherry and Chocolate Chip Oatmeal

One dish I make over and over in the pressure cooker is steel-cut oatmeal. It's hands-off and there's no scorching on the bottom of the pot when I get distracted and walk away for five minutes. For a flavorful rendition, combine dark chocolate with plump, fresh cherries. Serve with a dollop of plain or vanilla yogurt for a real breakfast treat. SERVES 4

Cooking spray or 1 teaspoon butter

1 cup steel-cut oats

3 cups water

¼ teaspoon salt

1 pinch grated nutmeg

2 tablespoons maple syrup

½ teaspoon vanilla extract

1 to 2 tablespoons brown sugar (optional)

½ cup semisweet or dark chocolate chips

1½ cups fresh cherries, halved and pitted

GREASE the bottom half of your Instant Pot with cooking spray or butter. Add the oats, water, salt, and nutmeg and stir. Secure the lid.

COOK at high pressure for 15 minutes and use a natural release.

ADD the maple syrup and vanilla and stir until creamy. Add brown sugar if you'd like your oatmeal sweeter (keep in mind that the chocolate and cherries will add some sweetness).

TOP each serving with chocolate chips and fresh cherries and serve.

P.S. If it isn't cherry season, replace the fresh cherries with ½ cup dried cherries.

Brown Butter and Pear Wheat Berry Bowl

It's time to get some new grains in your life, and there's no better time than breakfast. A bowl of nutty, chewy wheat berries is dressed with toasty brown butter, maple syrup, and cinnamon. Thinly sliced fresh pears add texture and fruity sweetness, and for an extra-complete breakfast, add a dollop of yogurt and a handful of toasted walnuts.   SERVES 4

1 cup wheat berries (hard or soft), rinsed and drained

4 cups water

1 teaspoon canola or grapeseed oil

½ teaspoon salt

3 tablespoons unsalted butter

2 to 3 tablespoons maple syrup

½ teaspoon ground cinnamon

2 ripe pears, cored and thinly sliced

½ cup plain or vanilla Greek yogurt (optional)

½ cup toasted walnuts (optional)

COMBINE the wheat berries, water, oil, and salt in your Instant Pot. Secure the lid.

COOK at high pressure for 30 minutes for soft/pearled berries, or 40 minutes for hard berries. Use a natural release.

CHECK for doneness. The berries should be chewy but not hard. Drain and rinse with cool water. While the berries drain, clean and dry the pot.

TURN on the Sauté function. Once hot, add the butter. Cook, swirling with a long-handled spoon, for 5 to 10 minutes, until the butter is lightly browned and smells toasty. Turn off the Sauté function and add the cooked wheat berries. Add the maple syrup (to taste) and cinnamon and toss well.

SERVE topped with pears and garnished with yogurt and walnuts (if using).

P.S. The dressed wheat berries keep for a few days in the fridge. When it's breakfast time, top with freshly sliced pear, yogurt, and walnuts (if using) for a quick, chilled breakfast.

Polenta and Soft-Boiled Eggs with Gremolata

With a little careful cooking, humble cornmeal can be transformed into creamy polenta. This Italian food staple is especially painless when made in the pressure cooker, emerging free of scorching and expertly cooked. Follow the directions to a T, and don't leave off the super simple but punchy gremolata. It's especially easy if you have a Microplane grater, which makes fast work of the lemon zest, garlic, and parmesan.   SERVES 4

3 cups water

4 large eggs

2 cups vegetable or chicken broth

I teaspoon olive oil

½ to I teaspoon salt, plus more for seasoning

I cup dried polenta

¼ cup packed finely chopped fresh parsley

I large lemon, zested, plus I teaspoon juice

I garlic clove, finely grated

I tablespoon butter

¼ cup grated parmesan cheese

ADD 1 cup water and a steamer basket or trivet to your Instant Pot. Place the eggs in the basket or on the trivet (not touching the sides). Secure the lid.

COOK at low pressure for 4 minutes and use a quick release. Carefully place the eggs in an ice water bath to cool. Wipe out the pot and place it back in the cooker.

ADD 2 cups water, the broth, oil, and ½ teaspoon table salt or 1 teaspoon kosher salt to the Instant Pot and turn on the Sauté function. Once simmering, add the polenta slowly while constantly whisking. Quickly secure the lid and turn off the Sauté function.

COOK at high pressure for 8 minutes. Use a natural release for 10 minutes followed by a controlled quick release.

WHILE the polenta is cooking, make the gremolata. In a small bowl, combine the parsley, lemon zest, lemon juice, and garlic. Season with salt and mix.

PEEL the cooled eggs, careful not to pierce the yolks.

ONCE the pressure has released, add the butter and parmesan and whisk vigorously until smooth. Add the gremolata and spoon into bowls. Top each with a soft-boiled egg cut in half and serve immediately.

P.S. All of the recipes in this book are best if you turn off the Keep Warm function, but it's especially important for this dish to avoid scorching.

Meaty Mains

Chicken and Olive Tagine

Hainanese Chicken Rice

Green Curry with Chicken, Eggplant, and Shishito Peppers

Chicken Mole

Easy Bo Ssam

Pork Chops and Rhubarb

Lazy Al Pastor

Andouille Sausage Pot Pie

Brats and Beets

Spicy Bolognese

Vietnamese Brisket Tacos

Beef Roast with Leeks and Turnips

Lamb Shanks with Red Chimichurri

Braised Short Ribs with Mushrooms

Nicoise Salad

Steamed Fish with Greens and Miso Butter

Chicken and Olive Tagine

Tagines are a North African dish that are named after the earthenware pot they're cooked in—meaning this is technically not a tagine. But for those of us not lucky enough to own a tagine, a pressure cooker will have to do! Chicken thighs are marinated in a fragrant blend of spices, which also flavor the reduced sauce at the end. The dish is a fantastic mix of tender chicken, warm spices, and briny olives. Serve with Ghee Mashed Potatoes (page 112) or a grain to soak up all of the rich sauce.

SERVES 4

2 teaspoons sweet paprika

1½ teaspoons ground cumin

1 teaspoon ground turmeric

½ teaspoon ground ginger

½ teaspoon ground cinnamon

4 large chicken thighs, skin-on and bone-in (2½ to 3 pounds)

Salt and pepper

2 tablespoons canola or grapeseed oil

1 onion, sliced

6 garlic cloves, smashed

2 tablespoons tomato paste

1 cup chicken broth

½ lemon, juiced

⅓ cup high-quality pitted olives

COMBINE the paprika, cumin, turmeric, ginger, and cinnamon in a small bowl. Season the chicken thighs generously with salt and pepper on both sides. Rub both sides of each thigh with the spice mixture, using it all. Place in a bowl or plastic bag to marinate for at least 1 hour or up to 3 hours.

ONCE the chicken is done marinating, turn on the Sauté function. Once hot, add the oil. Add 2 of the thighs, skin side down, and cook for about 3 minutes without moving. Remove and repeat with the remaining thighs. Set aside.

ADD the onion and cook for 2 minutes, scraping the bottom of the pot. Add the garlic and tomato paste and cook, stirring, for 1 more minute. Turn off the Sauté function. Add the broth and scrape any remaining bits off the bottom of the pot. Add the chicken, skin side up, and squeeze them in so that they fit in one layer. Secure the lid.

COOK at high pressure for 10 minutes and use a natural release.

REMOVE the chicken and some of the onions. Turn on the Sauté function and simmer the sauce for 10 to 15 minutes, until reduced by more than half and starting to thicken. Turn off the Sauté function. Add the lemon juice, stir, and taste for seasoning.

TO SERVE, pour the sauce over the chicken and sprinkle the olives on top.

Hainanese Chicken Rice

A fantastically simple dish, Chicken Rice appears in some form all over Asia. Bone-in, skin-on chicken cooks gently with aromatics, and its cooking liquid makes the rice pleasantly oily and savory. I buy my chicken already cut up into breasts, legs, wings, and thighs for ease. A bigger chicken will work, but you'll want to increase the water just enough so that most of the chicken is submerged.

SERVES 5 OR 6

FOR THE CHICKEN:

1 (3½-pound) chicken, cut into pieces

1½ teaspoons kosher salt, or 1 teaspoon table salt

½ small bunch scallions, cut into 2-inch-long pieces

1 (2-inch) piece of fresh ginger, sliced and lightly smashed

4 garlic cloves, smashed

3 cups water

FOR THE RICE AND SAUCE:

1 tablespoon canola or grapeseed oil

½ medium onion, diced

4 garlic cloves, minced

2 cups long-grain white rice, rinsed and drained well

½ small bunch scallions, sliced (dark green parts discarded)

1 (1-inch) piece of fresh ginger, peeled and grated or finely minced

2 tablespoons soy sauce

2 teaspoons sesame oil

Salt

2 medium cucumbers, peeled and sliced

¼ cup roughly chopped fresh cilantro

FOR THE CHICKEN: Season the chicken pieces on all sides with the salt. Add the chicken, scallions, ginger, and garlic to your Instant Pot. Add the water and push the chicken down so that it is mostly submerged. Secure the lid.

COOK at high pressure for 8 minutes and use a natural release.

DRAIN the cooked chicken, reserving all of the cooking liquid, and set aside to let rest. Discard the scallions, ginger, and garlic. Wipe out the pot.

FOR THE RICE: Turn on the Sauté function. Once hot, add the oil followed by the onion and cook for 1 minute. Add the garlic and rice and cook for 1 minute more, stirring. Turn off the Sauté function. Add 3 cups of the reserved cooking liquid and secure the lid.

COOK at high pressure for 3 minutes and use a natural release.

MAKE the sauce: In a small bowl, combine the scallions, ginger, soy sauce, sesame oil, 2 tablespoons of the reserved cooking liquid, and a pinch of salt.

DISCARD the chicken skin (this is optional). Once the pressure has released, fluff the rice and taste for seasoning.

SERVE with the cucumbers and sauce and top with cilantro.

Green Curry with Chicken, Eggplant, and Shishito Peppers

Coconut milk–based and packed with flavor, Green Curry with Chicken, Eggplant, and Shishito Peppers is quick and filling. Boneless chicken thighs are cooked whole to keep them moist, and shishito peppers are broiled separately for a smoky addition. Store-bought curry paste is elevated by fresh ginger, garlic, and lime, and the whole thing gets a kick in the pants from a potent little Thai chile. If you've ever cut up a hot pepper and rubbed your eye, then you know to proceed with caution here. I'd highly recommend wearing gloves. Leave it out if you're a wuss.

SERVES 3 OR 4

1 tablespoon plus 1 teaspoon coconut, canola, or grapeseed oil

1 small onion, thinly sliced

3 tablespoons green Thai curry paste

2 teaspoons peeled and grated fresh ginger

2 garlic cloves, minced

1 Thai or bird's-eye chile, minced

3 to 4 boneless, skinless chicken thighs (1¼ to 1½ pounds), excess fat removed

10 ounces Japanese eggplant, large diced (about 2 cups)

1 (14-ounce) can light coconut milk

Salt and pepper

6 ounces shishito peppers, stems removed and cut into 1-inch pieces (about 2 cups)

1 teaspoon sugar

½ lime, juiced

2 tablespoons chopped fresh cilantro, plus more for garnish

Cooked rice, for serving (optional)

PREHEAT your broiler.

TURN on the Sauté function. Once hot, add 1 tablespoon oil followed by the onion and sauté for 2 minutes. Add the curry paste, ginger, garlic, and chile and cook, stirring, for one minute. Turn off the Sauté function.

ADD the chicken thighs and spread out to form a layer over the onion. Add the eggplant and coconut milk and push the eggplant down so that most of it is covered in liquid. Season with salt and pepper. Secure the lid.

COOK at high pressure for 5 minutes and use a natural release.

MEANWHILE, toss the shishito peppers in 1 teaspoon oil and season with salt. Spread out on a small baking sheet and cook under your broiler, tossing once, until lightly browned and tender (about 5 minutes).

ONCE the pressure has been released, tear the chicken into large chunks. Add the sugar and lime juice and stir. Taste for seasoning. Add the shishito peppers and cilantro.

GARNISH with more cilantro and serve with rice (if using).

P.S. If you can't find skinless, boneless chicken thighs, buy the regular kind and do it yourself. Remove the skin and excess fat and flip over so that the smooth side that formerly had skin on it is facing down. Make a long cut from one end of the bone to the other. Pull back the meat to reveal the bone and cut around it using the tip of your knife. Remove the bone and trim off any cartilage remaining on the meat.

Chicken Mole

Mole is a popular Mexican sauce with endless variations, and often includes a long list of ingredients including chile peppers, spices, fruit, nuts, seeds, and more. My Chicken Mole is closest to a mole poblano, with dried ancho chiles, almonds, cumin, fire-roasted tomatoes, and a hint of chocolate. It's a streamlined take on the dish, but it has lots of spicy, sweet, and savory flavor. Serve with rice and beans, or make simple tacos with sliced avocado. SERVES 6 TO 8

3 pounds large boneless, skinless chicken breasts

5 garlic cloves, smashed

1 bay leaf

1 teaspoon salt, plus more for seasoning

2 cups chicken broth

1 tablespoon canola or grapeseed oil

1 small onion, finely diced

2 ounces dried ancho chiles, stemmed, seeded, and torn into pieces

¼ cup sliced almonds

¼ cup hulled pumpkin seeds (pepitas)

1 teaspoon ground cumin

½ teaspoon ground cinnamon

¼ teaspoon ground cloves

1 (14.5-ounce) can fire-roasted tomatoes, drained

1 heaping tablespoon raisins

Black pepper

2 ounces Mexican chocolate, chopped

ADD the chicken, 3 garlic cloves, the bay leaf, salt, and broth to your Instant Pot. Secure the lid.

COOK at high pressure for 5 minutes and use a natural release for 5 minutes followed by a quick release. Make sure the chicken is cooked through and remove, reserving the cooking liquid. Cover the chicken and set aside.

WHILE the chicken cools, wipe out the pot. Turn on the Sauté function. Once hot, add the oil followed by the onion. Sauté for 3 minutes. Add the chiles and cook for 2 minutes. Add the almonds, pumpkin seeds, cumin, cinnamon, and cloves and stir. Cook for 1 more minute and turn off the Sauté function.

ADD the tomatoes, raisins, and 1¼ cups of the reserved cooking liquid. Season with salt and pepper. Secure the lid.

COOK at high pressure for 10 minutes and use a natural release for 5 minutes followed by a quick release.

MEANWHILE, shred the chicken. Once the pressure has released, add the chocolate to the pot and stir until melted. Add the mixture to your blender and puree with the lid cracked. Taste the mole for seasoning.

TOSS the mole with the chicken and serve.

Easy Bo Ssam

Bo ssam is a delicious Korean boiled pork dish that's eaten wrapped in lettuce or cabbage and can have a myriad of toppings. Easy Bo Ssam is as promised, decidedly simplified but still impressive and fun to serve at a dinner party. I definitely recommend seeking out Korean soybean paste (doenjang), but miso will do in a pinch. Bo ssam is frequently served with oysters, and you can include them if you want to really take your dinner over the top. SERVES 6 TO 8

FOR THE PORK:

1 (3- to 3½-pound) bone-in pork shoulder

1 tablespoon kosher salt, or 2 teaspoons table salt

1 onion, cut into eighths

12 garlic cloves, smashed

1 (3-inch) piece fresh ginger, sliced

2 tablespoons doenjang (Korean fermented soybean paste) or miso paste

2 tablespoons sugar

5 cups water

FOR THE RICE:

1 teaspoon sesame oil

1 small bunch scallions, chopped, dark green tops discarded

⅔ cup long-grain white rice

1 cup water

Salt

FOR SERVING:

1 large head leaf lettuce (romaine, curly, or butter)

Kimchi

Gochujang (Korean chile sauce)

MAKE the pork: Salt all sides of the pork shoulder. Add it to your Instant Pot and top with the onion, garlic, ginger, doenjang, sugar, and water. Secure the lid.

COOK at high pressure for 1 hour and use a natural release.

MEANWHILE, make the rice: Heat a medium saucepan over medium heat. Add the sesame oil and scallions and cook for 1 minute. Add the rice, water, and a sprinkle of salt and bring to a boil. Reduce the heat to low and cover. Cook for 12 to 18 minutes, according to package directions, or until the water is absorbed and the rice is tender. Let sit, off the heat, for 5 minutes and then fluff with a fork.

DRAIN the pork and let rest for 5 to 10 minutes. Tear the meat into chunks, discarding the aromatics, excess fat, and the bone.

SEPARATE the lettuce leaves and wash and dry them. Serve the pork with the lettuce, rice, kimchi, and gochujang.

TO EAT, take a lettuce leaf and add pork, rice, kimchi, and a little gochujang and wrap it up like a taco.

Pork Chops and Rhubarb

When you see the words "pork chop," you might think pan-fried. But Pork Chops with Rhubarb are something else altogether, fall-off-the-bone and dressed in a luxurious sauce. Make sure you buy bone-in loin chops since boneless, less fatty chops will turn tough, and double everything (except the cook time) if you're feeding a crowd. SERVES 3

1 tablespoon butter

2 large bone-in pork loin chops (1¼ to 1½ pounds total)

Salt and pepper

1 small onion, sliced

½ cup chicken broth

12 ounces fresh rhubarb, sliced

3 cups packed sliced green cabbage

¼ cup honey

½ teaspoon Dijon mustard

½ teaspoon cornstarch

TURN on the Sauté function. Once hot, add the butter and let melt. Season the pork chops with salt and pepper on both sides and add to the pot in one layer. Let brown on one side for 2 minutes, then flip and brown the second side. Set aside.

ADD the onion to the pot and sauté for 2 minutes, scraping the bottom of the pot. Turn off the Sauté function. Add the broth and stir. Lay the pork chops on top. Secure the lid.

COOK at high pressure for 10 minutes and use a quick release.

ADD the rhubarb and cabbage and nestle them in around and under the pork chops. Secure the lid.

COOK at high pressure for 3 minutes and use a natural release.

REMOVE the pork chops, cabbage, rhubarb, and most of the onion with a slotted spoon. Tent with foil and set aside. Turn on the Sauté function. Once simmering, add the honey and mustard and stir. Sift in the cornstarch while stirring and cook for 5 minutes, or until slightly thickened. Taste the gravy for seasoning.

SERVE the pork chops and cabbage topped with the gravy.

Lazy Al Pastor

Al pastor is a shawarma-style Mexican dish, with layers of pork and pineapple shaved off a spit and served on tortillas. The lazy version is as advertised—it cooks largely unattended and there's no spit required, but it has all of the flavors you're looking for. You can break down the pork shoulder yourself or have a kind butcher do it. Remove the fat cap and any other big pieces, but leave the rest of the fat for flavor and tenderness. SERVES 6 TO 8

1 (3-pound) pork shoulder roast, cut into 1-inch cubes with excess fat removed

1 tablespoon chili powder

1 teaspoon ground cumin

½ teaspoon dried oregano

Salt and pepper

1 tablespoon canola or grapeseed oil

1 onion, sliced

8 garlic cloves, smashed

2 cups diced fresh pineapple

1 cup chicken broth

4 chipotle chiles in adobo, finely diced, plus 1 tablespoon adobo sauce

FOR SERVING:

Tortillas (corn or flour)

Avocado (optional)

Lime wedges (optional)

IN a large bowl, toss the pork with the chili powder, cumin, and oregano. Season generously with salt and pepper.

TURN on the Sauté function. Once hot, add the oil followed by the onion. Sauté for 3 minutes and add the garlic. Stir and turn off the Sauté function.

ADD the pineapple, broth, and chiles with adobo sauce to the pot and stir. Add the spiced pork and secure the lid.

COOK at high pressure for 20 minutes and use a natural release.

REMOVE the pork and pineapple with a slotted spoon. Turn on the Sauté function. Cook the sauce for about 30 minutes or until reduced by at least two-thirds. Turn off the Sauté function. Taste for seasoning and return the pork to the pot.

USE a slotted spoon to drain and serve the pork and pineapple in tortillas with avocado on top and lime wedges (if using).

P.S. The tacos are wet ones but so worth it. Just be sure to load up on napkins.

Andouille Sausage Pot Pie

A homemade pot pie bubbling away in the oven for an hour is well and good, but I love this shortcut: make a quick filling in the Instant Pot and a quick pastry in the oven and join them in holy matrimony at the end. Andouille sausage adds tons of smoky flavor, and store-bought puff pastry makes a super flaky topping with very little effort.   SERVES 4

1 (8.65-ounce) sheet frozen puff pastry

1 tablespoon plus 1 to 2 teaspoons canola or grapeseed oil

12 ounces andouille sausage, cut into ½-inch slices and then halved

½ onion, diced

2 shallots, diced

2 carrots, diced (about 1½ cups)

3 garlic cloves, minced

1 pound white or red potatoes, cut into ¾-inch cubes (about 3½ cups)

1½ cups chicken broth

Salt and pepper

1 tablespoon butter, slightly softened

2 tablespoons all-purpose flour

SET the puff pastry out on the counter to thaw for 30 minutes.

PREHEAT your oven to 400 degrees.

TURN on the Sauté function. Once hot, add 1 tablespoon oil followed by the sausage. Cook, stirring once or twice, for about 2 minutes, or until browned on at least one side.

REMOVE the sausage and set aside. Add 1 to 2 more teaspoons oil as needed. Add the onion and shallots and sauté for 2 minutes, scraping the bottom of the pot. Add the carrots and garlic and sauté for 1 minute more. Turn off the Sauté function. Add the potatoes, browned sausage, and broth. Season with salt and pepper and secure the lid.

COOK at high pressure for 7 minutes and use a natural release for 10 minutes followed by a quick release.

MEANWHILE, once the oven has preheated and the puff pastry is thawed, cut the sheet into four rectangles. Space 1 inch apart on a baking sheet. Bake for 10 to 20 minutes, following package directions, until nicely browned and flaky.

ONCE the pressure has released, turn on the Sauté function. Carefully remove and dispose of ½ cup of the broth, avoiding the onions when possible. Create a paste out of the butter and the flour and add to the pot. Stir and cook for about 3 minutes, until the mixture begins to thicken up. Taste for seasoning. Turn off the Sauté function and let cool for 5 to 10 minutes.

(continued)

ADD the pot pie mixture to 4 bowls or soup plates and serve topped with the baked puff pastry.

P.S. Swap out some of the potatoes for parsnips or butternut squash, or add a big handful of frozen peas at the end.

Brats and Beets

Beat on the brat! Beat on the brat! That's for all the pressure cooking Ramones fans out there. Brats and Beets is a simple combination of vibrant beets, their lightly bitter greens, juicy brats, and a bath of beer and broth (lots of B's). The beets turn the onion a deep red, and the flavors all marry together into an earthy and meaty dish. SERVES 3 OR 4

2 tablespoons canola or grapeseed oil

1 pound large uncooked bratwurst sausages (about 3)

1 red onion, sliced

1 (12-ounce) can or bottle lager-style beer

1 cup beef, chicken, or vegetable broth

Salt and pepper

1 pound beets, cut in half or quarters as needed so that the thickest part is 1½ inches thick, stems discarded, greens roughly chopped

¼ cup sour cream

2 teaspoons Dijon mustard

TURN on the Sauté function. Once hot, add the oil followed by the sausages. Brown on both sides, about 3 minutes per side. Remove and set aside.

ADD the onion to the pot and sauté for about 3 minutes, or until starting to brown. Add the beer and scrape the bottom of the pot, getting any brown bits. Turn off the Sauté function.

ADD the broth and season with salt and pepper. Add the sausages and beets and nestle them in. Add the greens on top. Secure the lid.

COOK at high pressure for 10 minutes and use a natural release for 10 minutes followed by a quick release.

IN a small bowl, combine the sour cream and mustard. Serve the Brats and Beets with the sauce on the side for dipping.

Spicy Bolognese

There's almost nothing more pleasing to the soul than a plate full of pasta covered in Bolognese. Little old Italian ladies will tell you that the sauce has to simmer for several hours, all day really, to get a deep flavor. Luckily, the Instant Pot can speed things up while keeping the sauce rich. I started with Marcella Hazan's classic recipe, tweaked it for the pressure cooker, and added a kick using spicy pork sausage and red pepper flakes. The sauce will keep for a few days if you have extra, but make the pasta fresh.   SERVES 4 TO 6

2 tablespoons butter

1 small onion, diced

2 celery ribs, diced

1 large carrot, diced

3 garlic cloves, minced

8 ounces ground beef chuck

8 ounces spicy pork sausage, without casing

¼ teaspoon red pepper flakes

Salt and pepper

½ cup dry white wine

1 (28-ounce) can Italian plum tomatoes, with juice, broken up into small pieces with a potato masher or by hand

1 bay leaf

½ cup heavy cream

1 pound dried or fresh pasta, such as fettuccine

Freshly grated parmesan cheese, for serving

TURN on the Sauté function. Once hot, add the butter followed by the onion, celery, carrot, and garlic. Sauté for 3 minutes. Add the beef and sausage and break up into small pieces, cooking until the meat is cooked through.

ADD the pepper flakes and season with salt and pepper. Add the wine and simmer for 10 minutes, or until almost all of the liquid is gone. Turn off the Sauté function. Add the tomatoes with juice and the bay leaf and stir. Secure the lid.

COOK at high pressure for 1 hour and use a natural release for 15 minutes followed by a quick release.

REMOVE the bay leaf. Skim off some of the oil on top (optional). Turn on the Sauté function to low. Add the cream and simmer with the lid off for 20 to 30 minutes, stirring occasionally to make sure it doesn't scorch on the bottom. The sauce will reduce by half and should be thick but not dry. Turn off the Sauté function.

WHEN the sauce is almost done, put a large pot of salted water on to boil. Cook the pasta according to the package directions and drain.

IMMEDIATELY add the pasta to the Bolognese and toss. Serve with parmesan.

Vietnamese Brisket Tacos

I live in Los Angeles, where we are very fortunate to have a number of food trucks and eateries that serve stand-in-line-worthy Vietnamese-Mexican fusion. Vietnamese tacos might seem like a weird combo, but just trust me. It's a match made in food heaven. Tender meat and crunchy veggies are dressed with savory, tangy, sweet, and salty ingredients for a happy marriage of flavors and textures—no waiting in line required. SERVES 4 OR 5

1 tablespoon sesame oil

1 small onion, sliced

4 garlic cloves, smashed

1 heaping tablespoon minced fresh ginger

1 (2- to 2½-pound) brisket, at room temperature

Salt and pepper

½ cup hoisin sauce

3 tablespoons fish sauce

2 tablespoons sriracha

¼ cup water

2 cups rainbow coleslaw mix

1 cucumber, cut into matchsticks

1 jalapeño, thinly sliced

2 tablespoons chopped fresh cilantro

1 tablespoon rice vinegar

½ lime, juiced

Tortillas, warmed, for serving

TURN on the Sauté function. Add the sesame oil followed by the onion. Sauté for 1 minute, add the garlic and ginger, and sauté for 2 more minutes. Turn off the Sauté function.

SEASON the brisket with salt and pepper on both sides and add to the pot. Top with the hoisin sauce, fish sauce, sriracha, and water. Secure the lid.

COOK at high pressure for 1 hour and use a natural release for 10 minutes followed by a quick release.

IN a medium bowl, combine the coleslaw mix, cucumber, jalapeño, cilantro, rice vinegar, and lime juice. Season with salt and pepper and toss together.

ONCE the pressure has released, remove the brisket to a cutting board and let rest. Turn on the Sauté function and boil the sauce for 10 minutes to thicken. Turn off the Sauté function. Slice the brisket into thin pieces against the grain, discarding any large pieces of fat. Return to the sauce.

TOP warmed tortillas with sauce-coated brisket and slaw and serve.

P.S. You can double this recipe if you have 4 to 5 pounds brisket. Simply cut your brisket in half so that it'll fit in the cooker and increase the cook time to 1½ hours.

Beef Roast with Leeks and Turnips

If you're hankering for a big piece of meat for Sunday supper, look no further. The roast is punched up with red wine and soy sauce, and creamy turnips replace the typical potatoes. The onion-leek gravy comes together quickly, and really puts the whole meaty dish over the top. Speaking of leeks, make sure yours are nice and clean. After chopping them up, soak them in a bowl of cold water and swish them around. After sitting for a few minutes, the dirt should sink to the bottom. Drain the leeks well before using.

SERVES 4 OR 5

1 (2-pound) beef chuck roast

Salt and pepper

¼ cup plus 1 tablespoon all-purpose flour

1 to 2 tablespoons canola or grapeseed oil

1 small onion, diced

2 large leeks, white and light green parts cut into ½-inch slices (discard dark green leaves)

½ cup red wine

1 cup beef or chicken broth

1 bay leaf

2 tablespoons soy sauce

1 teaspoon Worcestershire sauce (optional)

1 pound turnips, large diced

2 tablespoons chopped fresh parsley

TURN on the Sauté function to high. Season the roast with salt and pepper and coat with ¼ cup flour on all sides, tapping off the excess. Once hot, add 1 tablespoon oil to your Instant Pot followed by the roast. Brown on all sides for 3 to 4 minutes per side. Remove and set aside.

ADD another glug of oil to the pot if needed. Add the onion and leeks and sauté for 3 minutes. Season with salt and pepper. Add the wine and cook for 5 to 6 minutes, or until the wine is reduced by half and no longer smells like alcohol. Turn off the Sauté function.

PLACE the beef on top of the onion and leeks. Add the broth, bay leaf, soy sauce, and Worcestershire sauce (if using). Secure the lid.

COOK at high pressure for 1 hour and use a quick release.

ADD the turnips and push them down next to and under the roast so that they are mostly submerged. Secure the lid.

COOK at high pressure for 4 minutes and use a natural release for 10 minutes followed by a quick release.

ONCE the pressure has released, remove the meat to a plate and tent with aluminum foil to rest. Remove the veggies with a slotted spoon, leaving most of the onion and leeks behind. Discard the bay leaf.

TURN on the Sauté function to high. Once simmering, slowly sift 1 tablespoon flour into the gravy while whisking. Cook for about 5 minutes, until thickened and slightly reduced.

SERVE the roast and parsnips topped with the gravy and parsley.

P.S. Try pairing the roast with Creamed Collard Greens (page 116).

Lamb Shanks with Red Chimichurri

Chim chimminy, chim chimminy, chim chim chimichurri! I'm pretty sure Dick Van Dyke was singing about a flavorful Argentinian sauce that marries fresh herbs, garlic, spices, and vinegar and tastes great on meat. The red version adds red bell pepper and paprika for a complex albeit not-that-red sauce that is asking to be drizzled over tender lamb shanks. If you have trouble finding shanks, ask the butcher in your local grocery store to cut you some.

SERVES 3 OR 4

3 lamb shanks

Salt and pepper

2 tablespoons canola or grapeseed oil

1 onion, diced

5 garlic cloves, smashed

6 fresh thyme sprigs (optional)

½ cup red wine

1 (8-ounce) can tomato sauce

2 cups chicken or beef broth

1 red bell pepper, chopped

¼ cup fresh parsley leaves

2 tablespoons fresh cilantro leaves

1 tablespoon fresh oregano leaves

1 teaspoon smoked paprika

½ teaspoon red pepper flakes

1 tablespoon red wine vinegar

1 tablespoon fresh lemon juice

1 tablespoon olive oil

TURN on the Sauté function. Season the lamb shanks with salt and pepper on all sides. Once hot, add the oil followed by two of the shanks in a single layer. Let cook without moving for 4 to 5 minutes, until browned. Turn and brown for 4 to 5 minutes on the other side. Repeat with the remaining shank. Set aside.

ADD the onion to the pot and sauté for 2 minutes. Add 3 garlic cloves and sauté for 1 minute. Add the thyme (if using) and wine and simmer for 5 minutes, or until the alcohol smell has dissipated and the wine has reduced by half. Turn off the Sauté function.

ADD the tomato sauce and broth and scrape the bottom of the pot. Season with salt and pepper. Add the shanks and nestle them in so that they fit in a single layer. Secure the lid.

COOK at high pressure for 1 hour and use a natural release for 20 minutes followed by a quick release.

MEANWHILE, make the chimichurri: Add the bell pepper, parsley, cilantro, oregano, paprika, and pepper flakes to a small food processor. Pulse until chunky. Scrape down the sides and add the vinegar, lemon juice, and oil. Season with salt and pepper. Pulse

(continued)

until the mixture looks like a chunky pesto. If you don't have a food processor, finely mince all ingredients and combine.

SERVE the shanks with a drizzle of the cooking liquid and a heaping spoonful or two of the red chimichurri.

Braised Short Ribs with Mushrooms

When I think ribs, I think Fred Flintstone at the drive-in ordering ribs so big they make his car fall over. Braised Short Ribs with Mushrooms are a little more manageable (they're even called short). They're like barbecue ribs' elegant but still flavorful cousin, and they pair rather nicely with mashed potatoes.

3 pounds bone-in beef short ribs	½ teaspoon cayenne pepper
Salt and pepper	1½ cups red wine
2 tablespoons canola or grapeseed oil	½ cup beef or chicken broth
1 onion, sliced	6 fresh thyme sprigs
2 large celery ribs, chopped	1 fresh rosemary sprig
6 garlic cloves, smashed	10 ounces cremini mushrooms, sliced in half
1 teaspoon ground cumin	

TURN on the Sauté function. Season the short ribs with salt and pepper on all sides. Once hot, add the oil followed by half of the short ribs. Cook for 3 minutes without moving, then flip and brown the other side for 3 minutes. Remove and repeat with the remaining ribs. Set aside.

ADD the onion and sauté for 2 minutes. Add the celery and garlic and sauté for 1 minute. Add the cumin and cayenne and stir. Add the wine, bring to a boil, and simmer for 3 minutes. Turn off the Sauté function. Add the broth, thyme, and rosemary. Add the short ribs and nestle them into one layer. Secure the lid.

COOK at high pressure for 45 minutes and use a natural release for 15 minutes followed by a quick release.

USE tongs or a slotted spoon to remove the ribs to a platter and tent with foil. Turn on the Sauté function. Bring to a boil and simmer for 5 minutes. Add the mushrooms and cook, occasionally dunking them, for 10 minutes, or until tender.

SERVE the short ribs with the mushrooms and the sauce drizzled on top.

Nicoise Salad

There are countless variations of this fresh and filling French salad, but few are this convenient. Thanks to the Instant Pot and a steamer basket, you can cook the potatoes, green beans, tuna, and egg all at once. While these ingredients steam, put together the dressing and arrange the plates. Start to finish, you have a sophisticated meal in about 15 minutes.

SERVES 2

8 ounces medium red potatoes, quartered

1 cup water

8 ounces tuna steak, cut into two steaks (or two 4-ounce steaks)

Salt and pepper

6 ounces green beans

1 large egg

2 tablespoons finely chopped anchovies (optional)

½ small shallot, minced

½ lemon, juiced

1 teaspoon balsamic vinegar

½ teaspoon Dijon mustard

½ teaspoon honey

3 tablespoons olive oil

2 cups tightly packed lettuce

8 small radishes, quartered (about ½ cup)

⅓ cup Nicoise or Kalamata olives

ADD the potatoes and water to the bottom of your Instant Pot. Place your steamer basket on top. Place the tuna steaks on a small piece of parchment or aluminum foil and season with salt and pepper. Place on the steamer basket. Add the green beans and egg next to the tuna and spread out. Secure the lid.

COOK at low pressure for 4 minutes and use a quick release.

MEANWHILE, make the dressing: In a small mixing bowl, combine the anchovies (if using), shallot, lemon juice, vinegar, mustard, and honey. Season with salt and pepper and whisk. Add the oil slowly, whisking constantly.

ONCE the pressure has released, place the green beans in an ice water bath and drain the potatoes. Let cool for a few minutes. Add the egg to the ice water bath and remove and drain the beans. Once the egg has cooled, peel and cut in half. Break the tuna into large flakes.

TOSS the lettuce with half of the dressing. Place on a platter and arrange the potatoes, tuna, green beans, egg, radishes, and olives on top. Season everything with salt and pepper and serve with the remaining dressing.

Steamed Fish with Greens and Miso Butter

Miso is best known for its namesake soup, but the fermented soybean paste is a little more versatile than that. Thanks to Chef David Chang's flavor-mashing brain, we have the condiment miso butter—a simple mixture of miso paste and butter that's bursting with umami. Look for miso in Asian supermarkets, and slather the butter on the tender steamed fish and aromatic greens.

SERVES 2 OR 3

1 cup vegetable or chicken broth

1 (1-inch) piece of fresh ginger, peeled and cut into matchsticks

1 garlic clove, sliced

2 white fish fillets, such as tilapia (about 12 ounces total)

1 teaspoon soy sauce

Salt and pepper

1 tablespoon butter, at room temperature

1½ teaspoons miso paste

¼ lemon

1 bunch kale, tough stems removed and leaves torn (about 4 packed cups)

ADD the broth, ginger, and garlic to your Instant Pot. Place the trivet on top followed by a piece of aluminum foil. Place the fish fillets, side by side, on top of the foil, drizzle with soy sauce, and season with salt and pepper. Secure the lid.

COOK at low pressure for 7 to 10 minutes depending on the thickness of the fillets and use a quick release.

MEANWHILE, make the miso butter: Mix the butter and miso well in a small bowl and set aside.

ONCE the pressure has released, check the fish for doneness and carefully remove using the foil. Squeeze lemon juice over the fillets.

CAREFULLY remove the trivet. Turn on the Sauté function and, once simmering, add the kale. Cook for 1 to 2 minutes, until wilted, and turn off the Sauté function. Remove using tongs or a slotted spoon. Season with salt and pepper.

TOP the greens with the fish fillets and serve with miso butter.

Veggie Mains

Roasted Tomato and Feta Risotto

Farro "Fried Rice"

Chipotle Pinto Beans and Wild Rice

Charred Vegetable and Cheese Grits

White Bean Ragu Spaghetti

Red Curry with Kabocha Squash

Saag Tofu

Jackfruit Barbecue Sandwiches

Creamy Dal with Crispy Onions

Chickpeas with Spinach and Roasted Red Pepper

Vegetarian Stuffed Cabbage

Artichoke Heart and Lemony Pea Pasta

Biryani with Currants and Cashews

Tamale Pie

Parmesan Pumpkin Risotto

Roasted Tomato and Feta Risotto

If you're not using your Instant Pot to make risotto, then stop right there. You're having risotto for dinner. The cooker takes ordinary rice and turns it into a creamy, decadent dish and you barely have to stir. For a slightly different take on the traditional dish, I combine sweet roasted garlic and bursting tomatoes with salty feta and fresh chives. SERVES 4 TO 6

6 garlic cloves, unpeeled and whole, plus 4 garlic cloves, minced

2 teaspoons olive oil

1½ pounds grape or cherry tomatoes

4 tablespoons butter

1 large onion, diced

½ cup dry white wine

2 cups short-grain white rice

4½ cups vegetable broth

Salt and pepper

3 ounces crumbled feta cheese

2 tablespoons grated parmesan cheese

¼ cup chopped fresh chives

PREHEAT your oven to 400 degrees.

COAT the whole garlic cloves in ¼ teaspoon oil and place on a small piece of foil. Crumple the foil into a ball around the garlic, place in a small pan, and put in the oven. Bake for 5 minutes.

MEANWHILE, toss the tomatoes with the remaining oil on a baking sheet with sides. Once the garlic has been roasting for 5 minutes, add the tomatoes and cook both for 15 to 20 minutes, or until the tomatoes are all burst but not burnt. Let the garlic cool a bit before scraping out all of the roasted insides and mashing it into a paste.

MEANWHILE, turn on the Sauté function. Once hot, add the butter followed by the onion. Sauté for 3 to 4 minutes, until the onion is translucent. Add the minced garlic and cook for 1 minute. Add the wine and cook for 3 to 5 minutes, or until the alcohol smell has cooked off and the wine has reduced by half. Turn off the Sauté function. Add the rice and broth. Season with salt and pepper and stir. Secure the lid.

COOK at high pressure for 7 minutes and use a quick release.

ADD the mashed roasted garlic and stir well for a creamy texture. Add 2 ounces of the feta and the parmesan and stir. Taste for seasoning.

SERVE topped with the tomatoes, chives, and a sprinkle of feta cheese.

P.S. This recipe works well with short-grain brown rice, too. Follow the recipe as written except cook at high pressure for 25 minutes.

Farro "Fried Rice"

Using your Instant Pot and your stovetop, you can have "fried rice" in less time than the local Chinese restaurant delivers to your house. Mix things up by replacing the rice with farro, a healthy grain with a not-too-chewy texture. If you have leftover farro from another recipe, then even better. Switch out the veggies if you don't have one or two or simply don't like them—just be sure to include the garlic and ginger. SERVES 3 OR 4

1 cup semi-pearled farro	1 cup shelled edamame
2½ cups vegetable broth or water	3 garlic cloves, minced
1 teaspoon plus 3 tablespoons canola or grapeseed oil	2 teaspoons peeled and minced or grated fresh ginger
Salt and pepper	2 large eggs, beaten
1 small head broccoli, finely diced	1 cup fresh or frozen corn kernels
2 carrots, coarsely grated or finely diced	2 tablespoons soy sauce
1 small bunch scallions, thinly sliced	1 teaspoon toasted sesame oil

ADD the farro, broth, 1 teaspoon oil, and 1 pinch of salt to your Instant Pot. Secure the lid.

COOK at high pressure for 10 minutes and use a natural release. Drain completely and set aside to cool.

HEAT 1 tablespoon oil in a large skillet or wok over medium-high heat. Add the broccoli and carrots and cook, stirring, for 3 minutes. Add the scallions (reserving a handful for garnish) and edamame and cook, stirring, for 2 more minutes. Season with salt and pepper. Remove the veggies from the pan and set aside.

WIPE out the pan and add 2 tablespoons oil. Add the garlic and ginger and cook for 30 seconds, then add the cooked farro. Cook, stirring, for 3 minutes. Create a well in the middle, exposing the middle of the pan. Add the eggs and scramble them, then stir them into the farro. Add the corn and toss.

TURN the heat down. Add the veggies back to the pan and mix. Add the soy sauce and sesame oil and toss. Taste for seasoning and serve topped with raw scallions.

P.S. If you're a dedicated carnivore, you can add diced cooked chicken or pork to this recipe.

Chipotle Pinto Beans and Wild Rice

You know a pressure cooker is magic when it takes dry, hard-as-a-rock pinto beans and tough wild rice and cooks them up into a substantial meal in less than an hour. Chipotles add tons of smoky-spicy flavor, and the recipe is so filling you can get away with a one-dish dinner. It also makes a flavorful side for tacos like Lazy Al Pastor (page 43).   SERVES 4

8 ounces dried pinto beans, rinsed and drained

1 cup wild rice blend

2 tablespoons canola or grapeseed oil

1 teaspoon salt, plus more for seasoning

1 bay leaf

6 cups water

1 small onion, diced

1 small bell pepper, diced

2 garlic cloves, minced

2 chipotle chiles in adobo, minced, plus 2 tablespoons adobo sauce

ADD the beans, rice, 1 tablespoon oil, the salt, bay leaf, and water to your Instant Pot. Secure the lid.

COOK at high pressure for 30 to 35 minutes, depending on how old your beans are and how soft you like them. Use a natural release.

WHILE the pressure is releasing, add 1 tablespoon oil to a large skillet and preheat over medium heat. Add the onion and sauté for 2 minutes, then add the bell pepper and sauté for 3 more minutes, or until softened. Add the garlic and chipotles and cook for 2 more minutes. Add the adobo sauce, season with salt, and stir. Remove from the heat.

TASTE the beans and rice to make sure they are cooked through. If not, return to pressure for 3 to 5 minutes, until cooked through. Drain the beans and rice and remove the bay leaf. Add to the skillet and stir to incorporate the chipotle mixture. Taste for seasoning.

SERVE warm as a main dish or a side.

P.S. You can add greens to this meal and make it extra nutritious. Stir in a few cups of packed fresh spinach along with the bell pepper and cover the pan for 1 to 2 minutes to help the spinach wilt. Continue as written.

Charred Vegetable and Cheese Grits

Grits are a staple of southern cooking and require constant attention when cooking on the stovetop. Not so with the magic of pressure! Grits cook effortlessly before being spiked with sharp cheese, and a rainbow of charred vegetables brings texture and flavor to the party. Change up your vegetables as needed, but keep in mind that some veggies roast faster than others, so you may need to adjust your cook time.

SERVES 3 OR 4

1 cup coarse-ground grits

3 cups vegetable broth or water

2 tablespoons butter, cut into pieces

Salt and pepper

1 large head broccoli, stalk cut into ¼-inch pieces and top cut into medium florets

3 vine tomatoes, quartered

2 carrots, cut into ¼-inch coins

2 zucchini, cut in half from top to bottom, then cut into ½-inch slices

½ bell pepper, cut into 1-inch chunks

1 small bunch scallions, sliced into 1½-inch lengths, dark green ends discarded

4 large garlic cloves, cut into quarters

2 tablespoons canola or grapeseed oil

1 cup shredded white cheddar cheese

¼ to ½ cup milk

2 tablespoons chopped fresh parsley

Hot sauce, for serving

PREHEAT your oven to 425 degrees.

ADD the grits, broth, and butter to your Instant Pot, season with salt and pepper, and stir. Secure the lid.

COOK at high pressure for 15 minutes and use a natural release for 10 minutes followed by a quick release.

MEANWHILE, toss the broccoli, tomatoes, carrots, zucchini, bell pepper, scallions, and garlic with the oil and spread out in a single layer on a large baking sheet. Divide between two baking sheets if it's too crowded. Season with salt and pepper. Roast for 20 minutes, or until vegetables are tender but not mushy and are charred on the bottom.

ONCE the grits are finished cooking, add the cheese and whisk vigorously to break up any lumps. Add milk ¼ cup at a time until desired thickness is reached and season with salt and pepper as needed.

TOP with the vegetables followed by parsley and hot sauce (if using). Serve immediately.

(continued)

P.S. Add broiled shrimp on top of each portion for a dose of protein: Toss peeled shrimp in oil and season with salt and pepper. Broil for about 2 minutes on each side until pink on the outside and opaque all the way through.

White Bean Ragu Spaghetti

It may seem weird at first to put beans in pasta sauce, but creamy white beans will make a satisfying ragu for your next spaghetti dinner. Beans stew in vegetable broth and tomato until reduced for a flavor-packed, meatless pasta dish. The sauce is also superb eaten on top of toasted baguette or rustic bread with a drizzle of olive oil.   SERVES 3 OR 4

2 tablespoons olive oil

1 onion, diced

4 garlic cloves, minced

1 tablespoon tomato paste

1 cup dried white beans, preferably cannellini, presoaked and drained (see page 9)

3½ cups vegetable broth

1 bay leaf

1 (14.5-ounce) can diced tomatoes with juice, pureed

½ teaspoon dried oregano

¼ teaspoon red pepper flakes

Salt and pepper

12 ounces dried spaghetti, regular or whole wheat

Grated parmesan cheese, for serving

TURN on the Sauté function. Once hot, add the oil followed by the onion. Sauté for 2 minutes and add the garlic and tomato paste. Cook, stirring, for 1 minute. Turn off the sauté function. Add the presoaked beans, broth, and bay leaf and stir. Secure the lid.

COOK at high pressure for 8 minutes and use a natural release for 10 minutes followed by a quick release.

USING a measuring cup, remove ½ cup of the cooking liquid, avoiding the onion and beans as much as you can. Remove the bay leaf. Add the tomato puree, oregano, and pepper flakes to the pot. Season with salt and pepper.

TURN on the Sauté function to low and cook, uncovered, for about 20 minutes, stirring and scraping the bottom often to avoid scorching. The sauce will reduce by half and begin to thicken. Let cool for at least 5 minutes (it will thicken more as it sits) and taste for seasoning.

COOK the spaghetti according to the package directions and drain. Toss the pasta with the sauce and serve with parmesan.

Red Curry with Kabocha Squash

Kabocha squash is a Japanese variety that looks like a little green pumpkin and tastes kind of like butternut squash. Inspired by the culinary wizardry of J. Kenji López-Alt, I started adding the squash to my Thai-style curries with delicious results. It breaks down a bit during cooking, giving the coconut milk extra creaminess, and plays perfectly with the spicy red curry paste, crisp green beans, and tender bok choy. Try serving it with Sticky Rice (page 100).   SERVES 4

1 tablespoon coconut, canola, or grapeseed oil

1 small onion, thinly sliced

1 teaspoon grated fresh ginger

2 garlic cloves, minced

¼ cup red Thai curry paste

1 (14-ounce) can light coconut milk

⅓ cup vegetable broth

1 pound kabocha squash, peeled, seeded, and cut into 1-inch chunks (about 4 cups)

Salt and pepper

8 ounces fresh green beans, trimmed

1 small bell pepper, sliced

12 ounces bok choy, leaves separated and roughly chopped

1 (8-ounce) can sliced bamboo shoots

Fresh cilantro, for garnish (optional)

Cooked rice, for serving

TURN on the Sauté function. Once hot, add the oil followed by the onion and sauté for 2 minutes. Add the ginger and garlic and sauté for 1 minute. Add the curry paste and stir. Turn off the Sauté function.

ADD the coconut milk and broth and stir, scraping the bottom. Add the squash and season with salt and pepper. Secure the lid.

COOK at high pressure for 7 minutes and use a natural release for 10 minutes followed by a quick release.

TURN on the Sauté function and bring to a simmer. Add the green beans and bell pepper and simmer, loosely covered, for 3 minutes. Add the bok choy and bamboo shoots and simmer 1 more minute. Turn off the Sauté function and loosely cover. Let sit for 5 minutes.

TASTE for seasoning. Garnish with cilantro (if using) and serve with rice.

P.S. If you can't find kabocha squash, use butternut squash instead and reduce the cook time to 5 minutes.

Saag Tofu

Saag paneer is a vegetarian dish you'll find in many an Indian restaurant. Fragrant spices and aromatics cook with tender spinach and a mild, non-melty cheese called paneer. Don't get me wrong, paneer is delicious, but for a lighter version I replace it with firm tofu. Cauliflower and red bell pepper are added to bulk up the dish, and it's excellent served with toasted garlic naan or jasmine rice.

SERVES 4

14 ounces firm tofu, drained, cut into 1-inch cubes, and lightly pressed with paper towels to release excess moisture

1 teaspoon ground turmeric

1 teaspoon ground cumin

Salt and pepper

3 tablespoons canola or grapeseed oil

1 onion, finely chopped

6 garlic cloves, minced

1 tablespoon grated or finely minced fresh ginger

1 serrano or Thai chile, mostly seeded and finely diced

¾ cup vegetable broth

1 small red bell pepper, diced

2 teaspoons garam masala

12 ounces cauliflower, cut into small florets

1 pound fresh spinach, chopped

¼ to ⅓ cup Greek yogurt

1 tablespoon chopped fresh cilantro (optional)

ADD the tofu to a medium mixing bowl and sprinkle with turmeric and cumin. Season with salt and pepper. Gently toss to coat, careful not to break up the tofu.

TURN on the Sauté function. Once hot, add 2 tablespoons oil followed by the tofu. Cook for 2 to 3 minutes and toss, then cook for 2 to 3 minutes more. Return the cooked tofu to the bowl and set aside.

ADD 1 tablespoon oil to the pot. Add the onion and sauté for 2 minutes, scraping the bottom of the pot. Add the garlic, ginger, chile, and 2 tablespoons broth. Scrape the bottom of the pot. Sauté for 3 more minutes, periodically scraping the bottom of the pot, adding more broth if needed to prevent scorching.

ADD the bell pepper and garam masala and stir. Turn off the Sauté function. Add ½ cup broth and scrape the bottom of the pot one last time. Add the cauliflower followed by the spinach and season with salt and pepper. Secure the lid.

COOK at high pressure for 3 minutes and use a quick release.

TURN on the Sauté function. Add the cooked tofu and stir. Simmer for 5 minutes, stirring occasionally. Turn off the Sauté function and add ¼ cup yogurt. Stir and taste for seasoning, adding the remaining yogurt if desired.

SERVE topped with cilantro (if using).

P.S. Wear gloves when handling hot chiles! You can leave all of the seeds in if you like spicy stuff.

Jackfruit Barbecue Sandwiches

Jackfruit is a giant, bumpy fruit from south Asia that has, in recent years, become a popular meat substitute in the United States. The unripe fruit is mild and has a texture amazingly similar to pulled pork. Toss it in some barbecue sauce and add a little coleslaw and you've got yourself a mighty fine sandwich. Serve with oven fries or potato salad. SERVES 4

2 (20-ounce) cans young green jackfruit in water

1 tablespoon canola or grapeseed oil

Salt and pepper

1 cup ketchup

⅓ cup apple cider vinegar

¼ cup brown sugar

1 teaspoon Dijon mustard

1 teaspoon smoked paprika

1 teaspoon ground cumin

1 cup vegetable broth

3 cups packed coleslaw mix

2 tablespoons mayonnaise or vegan mayonnaise

4 hamburger buns

RINSE the jackfruit and drain, using a paper towel to lightly press out some of the excess moisture. Remove the tough cores with a knife and any seeds you can get to.

TURN on the Sauté function. Once hot, add the oil followed by the jackfruit. Sauté for 3 minutes and season with salt and pepper. Remove and set aside. Clean out the pot, dry, and return it to the cooker. Turn the Sauté function down to low.

ADD the ketchup, vinegar, brown sugar, mustard, paprika, and cumin. Season with salt and pepper and simmer for 4 minutes. Very loosely cover with the lid if the sauce starts to bubble outside the pot. Turn off the Sauté function. Remove ½ cup of the barbecue sauce and set aside.

ADD the broth and stir. Add the jackfruit and stir. Secure the lid.

COOK at high pressure for 10 minutes and use a natural release.

MEANWHILE, make the slaw: In a medium-sized mixing bowl, combine the coleslaw mix and mayonnaise. Season with salt and pepper and toss together.

ONCE the pressure has released, drain the jackfruit and discard the cooking liquid. Return it to the pot and use a fork to shred. Add all but a couple of tablespoons of the reserved barbecue sauce and toss.

TO SERVE, spread a small amount of barbecue sauce on both sides of each hamburger bun. Fill with the jackfruit followed by coleslaw.

Creamy Dal with Crispy Onions

Unlike other lentils, red lentils easily cook down to a creamy consistency, made all the more easy with a pressure cooker. Dal is colorful, fragrant, and vegetarian friendly. It's also filling, and paired with pita bread and a cucumber salad, you've got a whole meal. Speaking of cucumber salad: Combine 4 thinly sliced Persian cucumbers, ¼ thinly sliced red onion, juice of ½ lemon, 1 chopped fresh dill sprig, and salt and pepper.

SERVES 4

2 tablespoons ghee or butter

½ onion, finely diced, plus ½ onion, thinly sliced

1 heaping cup peeled and finely diced sweet potato

4 garlic cloves, smashed

1 tablespoon grated fresh ginger

4 teaspoons curry powder

½ teaspoon ground turmeric

¼ teaspoon red pepper flakes

1 cup red lentils, rinsed and picked over

2 roma tomatoes, finely diced

2 cups vegetable broth or water

3 tablespoons canola or grapeseed oil

2 tablespoons all-purpose flour

Salt and pepper

¼ cup plain yogurt

Fresh cilantro, chopped, for serving (optional)

Pita bread, for serving

TURN on the Sauté function. Once hot, add the ghee followed by the diced onion. Sauté for 2 minutes. Add the sweet potato, garlic, ginger, curry powder, turmeric, and pepper flakes. Cook, stirring and scraping the bottom, for 2 minutes. Turn off the Sauté function. Add the lentils, tomatoes, and broth and stir. Secure the lid.

COOK at high pressure for 10 minutes and use a natural release.

MEANWHILE, heat the oil in a large skillet over medium-high heat. Toss the sliced onion in the flour. Once hot, add the onion to the oil and fry for 3 to 4 minutes, flipping halfway, or until golden brown. Depending on the size of your pan, you may need to fry in two batches. Remove to a paper towel to drain and sprinkle with salt.

ONCE the pressure has released, season the dal with salt and pepper and add the yogurt. Stir vigorously with a spoon or whisk to achieve a creamy texture.

SERVE topped with cilantro (if using) and crispy onions and with warm pita on the side for scooping.

P.S. Use coconut oil instead of ghee/butter and leave out the yogurt for a vegan meal.

Chickpeas with Spinach and Roasted Red Pepper

Chickpeas are transformed from mere beans into a main dish with the help of smoky pepper and leafy spinach. Basil adds freshness, balsamic vinegar adds depth, and parmesan adds a salty bite. If you have roasted red peppers on hand, then ignore that part and simply dice and add to the mix. This dish is even better served warm with toasted or grilled bread.

SERVES 4

8 ounces dried chickpeas, presoaked and drained (see page 9)

2 garlic cloves, smashed, plus 2 garlic cloves, minced

1 teaspoon canola or grapeseed oil

½ teaspoon salt, plus more for seasoning

1 bay leaf

4 cups vegetable broth or water (or a combination)

1 large red bell pepper, seeded and stemmed and cut into 4 chunks, or 1 large roasted red pepper, seeded, peeled, and diced

3 teaspoons olive oil

1 large tomato, diced

1 bunch spinach, chopped, with large stems removed

1 teaspoon balsamic vinegar

3 tablespoons grated parmesan cheese, plus more for serving

2 tablespoons chopped fresh basil

Slices of baguette or rustic loaf, toasted (for serving)

PREHEAT your oven to 450 degrees.

ADD presoaked chickpeas, smashed garlic, canola oil, salt, and bay leaf to your Instant Pot. Add the broth. Secure the lid.

COOK at high pressure for 15 minutes and use a natural release.

IF you are roasting your own pepper: Coat the bell pepper in 1 teaspoon olive oil and sprinkle with salt. Place on a baking sheet and roast for about 25 minutes, turning once, until the skin is wrinkly and the pepper is charred. Remove from the pan, cover, and let cool. Once the pepper is cool enough to handle, peel off the skin and dice.

ONCE the pressure has released, taste the chickpeas for doneness. If not yet cooked through, return to pressure for 5 minutes.

(continued)

DRAIN the chickpeas, reserving ½ cup of the cooking liquid. Remove the bay leaf. Clean out the pot, dry, and return it to the cooker.

TURN on the Sauté function. Once hot, add 2 teaspoons olive oil. Add the minced garlic and cook for 30 seconds. Add the roasted pepper, tomato, spinach, drained chickpeas, and the reserved cooking liquid. Season with salt. Cook, stirring occasionally, for 5 minutes.

TURN off the Sauté function. Add the vinegar, parmesan, and basil and toss. Taste for seasoning.

TOP with more parmesan and serve with toasted bread.

Vegetarian Stuffed Cabbage

Stuffed cabbage (aka cabbage rolls) is a labor of love and a real homemade treat. I cut a few corners to save some time and steps, but the result is still an ultra-satisfying home-cooked meal. Ground beef is replaced by a mixture of wild rice and mushrooms, and the tomato and red pepper sauce just cooks once along with the rolls. The cabbage becomes tender and mild, and fresh herbs and paprika add a punch of flavor to the dish. If you can't find fresh marjoram, use fresh oregano instead.

SERVES 4

FOR THE CABBAGE ROLLS:
I tablespoon olive oil
½ large onion, diced
½ green bell pepper, diced
10 ounces cremini mushrooms, diced
3 garlic cloves, minced
I tablespoon tomato paste
I teaspoon chopped fresh thyme
I teaspoon chopped fresh marjoram
I¼ cups vegetable broth
½ cup wild rice mix
Salt and pepper
I small head green cabbage
½ cup panko breadcrumbs

FOR THE SAUCE:
I tablespoon olive oil
½ large onion, diced
½ red bell pepper, diced
2 garlic cloves, minced
Up to ½ cup vegetable broth
I½ teaspoons smoked or sweet paprika
I teaspoon sugar
Salt and pepper
I (28-ounce) can diced tomatoes, with juice, pureed

FOR THE CABBAGE ROLLS: Turn on the Sauté function. Once hot, add the oil followed by the onion and green bell pepper. Sauté for 2 minutes and add the mushrooms and garlic. Cook for 2 more minutes and turn off the Sauté function.

ADD the tomato paste, thyme, and marjoram. Stir well. Add the broth and rice, stir, and season with salt and pepper. Secure the lid.

COOK at high pressure for 25 minutes and use a natural release for 10 minutes followed by a quick release.

MEANWHILE, put a large pot of water on to boil. Cut off the stalk end of the cabbage and separate the leaves. Set aside the small, middle leaves to use for another recipe. Cut off any especially thick parts.

ONCE the water is boiling, add the cabbage leaves in two batches, boiling for just 2 minutes and then moving them to an ice water bath to cool. Drain well.

ONCE the pressure has released, drain the rice mixture, reserving the excess cooking liquid. Add the breadcrumbs to the rice and taste for seasoning.

PLACE a big spoonful of the rice mixture into a cabbage leaf and roll up. Place on a plate and repeat until the rice mixture is gone.

FOR THE SAUCE: Clean out the pot. Turn on the Sauté function. Once hot, add the oil followed by the onion and red bell pepper. Sauté for 2 minutes. Add the garlic and stir. Turn off the Sauté function.

ADD enough broth to the rice cooking liquid to make ⅔ cup and add to the pot. Add the paprika and sugar and season with salt and pepper. Stir. Add the cabbage rolls, seam side down, and nestle them into the sauce. Pour the tomato puree on top. Secure the lid.

COOK at high pressure for 10 minutes and use a natural release.

TO SERVE, spoon a few cabbage rolls onto each plate. Stir the sauce and spoon it over top.

Artichoke Heart and Lemony Pea Pasta

Artichokes are tricky veggies that always involve a lot of prep, but they are worth it for their buttery texture and mild flavor. This dish gets down to the heart of the matter, using the most edible and delicious part of the vegetable and combining it with fresh green peas and lots of garlic and lemon. If you're confused about how to trim the artichokes, I highly suggest looking at some photos or a video online. It's easier than it sounds. SERVES 2 OR 3

2 lemons, juiced, plus 1 lemon, zested and juiced

2 globe artichokes

10 ounces dried linguine or spaghetti

Salt

3 tablespoons olive oil

2 garlic cloves, minced

1 cup fresh green peas

¼ cup vegetable broth or water

3 tablespoons grated parmesan cheese, plus more for serving

1 tablespoon chopped fresh parsley

¼ teaspoon red pepper flakes

Pepper

PREPARE the artichokes: Fill a small bowl with cool water and the juice of 1 lemon. Start by snapping off all of the outer leaves until you're just left with the inner yellow leaves. Trim the nubs left behind by the outer leaves with a paring knife. Trim off the bottom inch of the stem and peel off the exterior of the stem to reveal the yellow interior. Trim the remaining leaves off with a sharp knife so that they are flush with the base of the artichoke. Drop the trimmed artichoke in the lemon water and repeat with the other artichoke.

PLACE both prepared artichokes and their lemon water in your Instant Pot. Add enough water, if needed, so that the artichokes barely float. Add the juice of 1 lemon. Secure the lid.

COOK at high pressure for 10 minutes and use a quick release.

MEANWHILE, cook the linguine in salted water according to the package directions and drain.

ONCE the pressure has released, remove the artichokes and let them cool a bit. Clean the pot. Once the artichokes are cool enough to handle, remove any remaining leaves to expose the choke. Scoop all of the feathery and tough bits out and discard. Chop the remaining tender hearts.

(continued)

TURN on the Sauté function. Once hot, add the oil followed by the garlic. Sauté for 30 seconds and add the peas and broth. Simmer for 2 minutes and turn off the Sauté function. Add the artichokes, parmesan, zest, and juice of 1 lemon, parsley, and pepper flakes. Season with salt and pepper.

ADD the pasta and toss. Serve topped with more parmesan.

Biryani with Currants and Cashews

Biryani, a fragrant mix of spices and rice, is a very popular dish in India, Pakistan, and the rest of South Asia. The aromatics, spices, veggies, and meat can all vary according to the region and the cook, but all versions of biryani layer flavor after flavor into fluffy basmati rice for a gratifying meal. You can add roasted or sautéed vegetables or meat after cooking for your own spin on the dish.　　　　　　　　　　　　　　　　　　　SERVES 4

2 tablespoons canola or grapeseed oil

2 large serrano chiles, whole

2 bay leaves

I small cinnamon stick

5 green cardamom pods, lightly smashed

½ teaspoon fennel seeds

½ teaspoon coriander seeds

I large onion, diced

4 garlic cloves, minced

2 teaspoons grated fresh ginger

I tomato, diced

I large carrot, finely diced

I small green or red bell pepper, diced

⅓ cup chopped fresh mint leaves

⅓ cup chopped fresh cilantro leaves, plus more for garnish

1½ teaspoons garam masala

½ teaspoon ground turmeric

I pinch saffron (5 to 6 threads; optional)

1¾ cups vegetable or chicken broth

I tablespoon plain yogurt

I tablespoon ghee or butter

Salt and pepper

1½ cups basmati rice, rinsed and drained well

½ cup frozen peas

⅓ cup dried currants

⅓ cup toasted cashew pieces

TURN on the Sauté function. Once hot, add the oil followed by the chiles, bay leaves, cinnamon stick, cardamom, fennel, and coriander. Sauté for 4 minutes and remove the cardamom pods. Add the onion and sauté for 3 minutes. Add the garlic and ginger and cook for 1 minute, stirring constantly.

ADD the tomato, carrot, bell pepper, mint, cilantro, garam masala, turmeric, and saffron (if using). Sauté for 1 minute and turn off the Sauté function.

ADD the broth, yogurt, and ghee. Stir and season with salt and pepper. Add the rice on top, pushing down just enough so that it is submerged in the broth; don't stir. Add the peas and currants on top. Secure the lid.

COOK at high pressure for 4 minutes and use a natural release for 10 minutes followed by a quick release.

REMOVE the chiles, bay leaves, and cinnamon stick. Add the cashews and fluff the rice. Let sit for at least 5 minutes, then garnish with cilantro and serve.

Tamale Pie

Tamale pie is a southwestern dish that marries the Mexican tamale with the all-American casserole. Many versions have a basic cornbread on top that crisps up in the oven, but I love the dense but fluffy texture of real masa. Make sure you leave a bit of gap at the edge between the topping and the filling, and let it cool for a while so that the masa can firm up. SERVES 4 OR 5

2 cups masa harina (labeled for tamales)

1 teaspoon salt plus more for seasoning

2⅔ cups vegetable or chicken broth

½ cup lard or shortening

1 teaspoon baking powder

1 tablespoon canola or grapeseed oil

1 onion, diced

1 green bell pepper, diced

1 large poblano pepper, diced

3 garlic cloves, minced

1 tablespoon tomato paste

1 tablespoon chili powder

1 teaspoon ground cumin

1 (14.5-ounce) can diced fire-roasted tomatoes, with juice, with or without chiles

2 (15-ounce) cans black beans, rinsed and drained

¾ cup shredded Monterey Jack or cheddar cheese

IN a medium mixing bowl, mix together the masa and salt. Add 2 cups broth and mix until fully incorporated.

BEAT the lard and baking powder until creamy with an electric mixer (about 1 minute). Add the masa mixture a spoonful at a time until incorporated, then beat on high for 5 minutes until fluffy.

TURN on the Sauté function. Once hot, add the oil followed by the onion. Sauté for 2 minutes. Add the bell pepper, poblano pepper, and garlic. Sauté for 3 minutes. Add the tomato paste, chili powder, and cumin and sauté for 1 minute. Turn off the Sauté function. Add the tomatoes, beans, and ⅔ cup broth and season with salt. Stir. Top with the cheese.

SPOON the masa mixture on top and spread out to create an even layer, leaving a small gap between the masa and the sides of the pot. Secure the lid.

COOK at high pressure for 25 minutes and use a natural release.

REMOVE the lid, careful not to drip any condensation onto the pie. Let cool for at least 10 minutes to let the masa firm up, then serve.

P.S. Note that lard is not vegetarian, so be sure to use shortening if you're eating totally veg.

Parmesan Pumpkin Risotto

When roasted, pumpkin becomes creamy and lightly sweet, playing off the saltiness of the parmesan cheese. Half of the pumpkin continues to cook with the rice, dissolving into the risotto, while half is diced and added at the end. If you have a bigger pumpkin, roast the whole thing and puree the extra for baking. Serve alongside a crunchy green salad with a lemony dressing.

SERVES 4

1 (2-pound) baking pumpkin (such as a sugar pumpkin)

2 teaspoons canola or grapeseed oil

Salt and pepper

4 tablespoons butter

1 onion, diced

4 garlic cloves, minced

½ cup dry white wine

3¼ cups vegetable or chicken broth

1½ cups short-grain white rice

1 teaspoon fresh thyme leaves, plus more for garnish

¾ cup grated parmesan cheese, plus more for serving

PREHEAT your oven to 400 degrees.

PREPARE the pumpkin: Cut off the stem and the very top of the pumpkin. Cut in half from top to bottom and scoop out all of the seeds and stringy innards. Cut into 3-inch slices. Place on a large baking sheet, skin side down, and rub with oil. Season with salt and pepper.

ROAST the pumpkin for about 40 minutes, or until tender. Once cool enough to handle, peel all the slices and dice.

TURN on the Sauté function. Once hot, add the butter followed by the onion. Sauté for 3 minutes, or until the onion is translucent. Add the garlic and cook for 1 minute. Add the wine and cook for about 4 minutes, or until the alcohol smell has cooked off and the wine has reduced by half. Turn off the Sauté function.

ADD the broth, rice, and thyme. Add half of the cooked diced pumpkin. Season with salt and pepper and stir. Secure the lid.

COOK at high pressure for 7 minutes and use a quick release.

ADD the parmesan and stir vigorously to break up the pumpkin and achieve a creamy texture. Taste for seasoning and let cool for a few minutes to thicken up.

SERVE topped with the reserved roasted pumpkin, more parmesan, and a sprinkle of thyme leaves.

Grainy and Beany Sides

Forbidden Rice with Grapefruit and Jalapeño

Zesty Refried Black Beans

Chorizo Hominy Grits

Cheesy Rice and Baby Broccoli

Beans 'n' Pork

Farro with Mixed Herb Pesto

Israeli Couscous Salad

Boston Brown Bread

Creamy Cauliflower and White Cheddar Rotini

Giant White Beans and Romesco

Sticky Rice

Chinese Five-Spice Black-Eyed Peas

Quinoa Salad with Edamame and Corn

Barley and Sugar Snap Pea Salad

Bleu Cheese and Caramelized Onion Polenta

Boiled Peanuts

Forbidden Rice with Grapefruit and Jalapeño

Forbidden rice (aka black rice) is extra-nutritious with a just-chewy-enough texture, but I'm really not supposed to talk about it (it's forbidden). The simple side dish gets a nice hit of umami from fish sauce, fruity bitterness from grapefruit, and a little crunch from fresh jalapeño. If you like things spicy, leave the seeds in your jalapeño. SERVES 3 OR 4

1 cup forbidden/black rice, rinsed and drained

1⅓ cups water

1 teaspoon canola, grapeseed, or olive oil

Salt

1½ teaspoons fish sauce

1 pinch sugar

1 grapefruit, peeled and segmented

1 jalapeño, seeded and finely diced

2 tablespoons chopped fresh cilantro

ADD the rice, water, oil, and a pinch of salt to your Instant Pot. Secure the lid.

COOK at high pressure for 24 minutes and use a natural release for 10 minutes followed by a quick release.

ADD the fish sauce and sugar and stir. Taste for seasoning. Add the grapefruit, jalapeño, and cilantro and toss. Serve.

P.S. This side dish pairs amazingly well with fish. Try it with Steamed Fish with Greens and Miso Butter (page 56).

Zesty Refried Black Beans

Refried beans are so tasty in burritos, tacos, or as a worthy side dish next to rice. They also make an awesome dip for tortilla chips, especially with a little melted cheese on top. Since you're pureeing everything at the end, don't make extra work for yourself by presoaking the beans. Double the recipe if you're serving a crowd. SERVES 4 OR 5

1 tablespoon canola or grapeseed oil

½ onion, cut into 1-inch chunks

2 garlic cloves, smashed

8 ounces dried black beans, rinsed and drained

4 cups vegetable broth or water (or a combination)

1 bay leaf

1 teaspoon salt, plus more to taste

½ teaspoon cayenne pepper, or more to taste

1 lime, zested and juiced

TURN on the Sauté function. Once hot, add the oil followed by the onion. Let sit for 1 to 2 minutes, until lightly charred. Add the garlic and turn off the Sauté function. Add the beans, broth, bay leaf, and salt. Secure the lid.

COOK for 35 minutes at high pressure and use a natural release.

CHECK the beans for doneness—they should be very tender. Drain the beans, garlic, and onion and reserve the cooking liquid. Remove the bay leaf.

ADD the beans, garlic, and onion back to the pot and add the cayenne, lime zest, and lime juice. Add ¼ cup of the reserved cooking liquid to start and use a blender, potato masher, or immersion blender to puree the bean mixture until you reach your desired consistency. Add more cooking liquid as needed. Season with salt to taste.

SERVE warm as a side dish or dip.

P.S. This recipe also works with pinto beans!

Chorizo Hominy Grits

Grits can get a bad rap as bland mush, but they often go under-seasoned and under-loved. Think of corn grits as a blank culinary canvas, upon which flavorful chorizo and chewy hominy play. And don't forget the cheese (duh). SERVES 4 OR 5

1 cup coarse-ground grits

4 cups vegetable or chicken broth or water (or a combination)

2 tablespoons butter, cut into pieces

Salt and pepper

1 tablespoon canola or grapeseed oil

1 small bunch scallions, chopped, dark greens reserved for garnish

1 garlic clove, minced

8 ounces Mexican uncooked chorizo or soy chorizo

1½ cups cooked or canned hominy, rinsed and drained

1 tablespoon chopped fresh oregano

⅓ cup shredded Monterey Jack or mild cheddar cheese

ADD the grits, 3½ cups broth, and butter to your Instant Pot, season with salt and pepper, and stir. Secure the lid.

COOK at high pressure for 15 minutes and use a natural release for 10 minutes followed by a quick release.

MEANWHILE, heat the oil over medium heat in a medium skillet. Once hot, add the chopped white and light green scallions and the garlic. Sauté for 1 minute. Remove the chorizo from the casing and add to the pan. Cook meat chorizo for 3 minutes while crumbling (or until mostly cooked through), or cook soy chorizo for 1 minute while crumbling. Add the hominy, oregano, and ½ cup broth and cook for 3 more minutes, or until the chorizo is completely cooked and most of the liquid has evaporated. Season with salt and pepper.

ONCE the pressure has released, add the cheese to the grits and whisk vigorously to break up any lumps. Season with salt and pepper as needed. Top with the chorizo mixture and serve immediately.

Cheesy Rice and Baby Broccoli

Broccoli and cheese is a classic combo that's always been a favorite of mine. The dish gets its cheesiness from Gruyère and parmesan, two cheeses that are strong enough that a little goes a long way. Baby broccoli has a crisper texture and milder flavor than regular old broccoli, and it works great with the creamy rice. Top with grilled chicken and some cooked carrots, peppers, or tomatoes to make it a main dish.

SERVES 4 OR 5

1 tablespoon plus 2 teaspoons olive oil

½ onion, diced

1½ cups long-grain brown or white rice, rinsed and drained

3 cups vegetable or chicken broth

Salt

12 ounces baby broccoli, stems cut into 1-inch pieces and florets separated

¼ cup water

2 garlic cloves, minced

⅓ cup milk

2 tablespoons sour cream

½ cup shredded Gruyère cheese

¼ cup grated parmesan cheese

TURN on the Sauté function. Once hot, add 1 tablespoon oil followed by the onion. Sauté for 2 minutes and turn off the Sauté function. Add the rice and stir. Add the broth and a healthy pinch of salt and secure the lid.

FOR brown rice, cook at high pressure for 23 minutes. For white rice, cook at high pressure for 4 minutes. Use a natural release.

MEANWHILE, cook the baby broccoli: Heat a large skillet over medium heat. Once hot, add the broccoli stems and water. Loosely cover and cook for 2 minutes. Add the florets, loosely cover, and cook for 1 minute more.

UNCOVER and cook off any remaining water. Add 2 teaspoons oil and the garlic. Season with salt. Sauté for about 3 minutes until tender but not overcooked. Remove from the heat.

ONCE the pressure has released, stir the rice. Add the milk, sour cream, and cheeses and stir well. Taste for seasoning. Add the broccoli and garlic on top and serve.

Beans 'n' Pork

You can't have a summer barbecue without baked beans, and no canned good can compare to homemade Beans 'n' Pork. Smoked bacon lends the side dish tons of flavor, and a simple sauce of ketchup, molasses, chili powder, and lemon juice is tangy, sweet, and smoky. Navy beans are the standard for this dish, but you can substitute Great Northern beans if needed.

SERVES 4 OR 5

I teaspoon canola or grapeseed oil

4 ounces thick-cut bacon, diced (about 2 strips)

½ onion, finely diced

3 garlic cloves, minced

I½ teaspoons chili powder

I½ cups chicken or vegetable broth

8 ounces dried navy beans, presoaked and drained (see page 9)

I bay leaf

Salt and pepper

¼ cup ketchup

2 tablespoons molasses

2 teaspoons fresh lemon juice

TURN on the Sauté function. Once hot, add the oil followed by the bacon. Sauté for 2 minutes, until starting to crisp. Add the onion and sauté for 3 minutes. Add the garlic and chili powder and sauté for 1 minute. Turn off the Sauté function.

ADD the broth and scrape the bottom of the pot well. Add the presoaked beans and bay leaf and season with salt and pepper. Secure the lid.

COOK at high pressure for 20 minutes and use a natural release for 10 minutes followed by a quick release.

REMOVE the bay leaf. Turn on the Sauté function to low. Add the ketchup and molasses and simmer, stirring occasionally, for 15 minutes, or until the beans are tender and the sauce has thickened. Add the lemon juice and taste for seasoning. Serve warm.

Farro with Mixed Herb Pesto

Farro is an ancient grain that has great texture, flavor, and nutrition, but can be a bit confusing to buy at the store. Often packages are merely labeled "farro," without specifying whether they are whole, semi-pearled, or pearled. The best way to find out is to check the cooking instructions—if it says to simmer the farro for 30 or so minutes, then bingo! You've got semi-pearled. Serve this vibrant dish with grilled shrimp, fish, or roasted chicken, or toss it with other veggies and eat it as a salad. SERVES 4 TO 6

1½ cups semi-pearled farro

3 cups vegetable broth or water (or a combination)

1 teaspoon canola or grapeseed oil

Salt

1 cup packed fresh basil

½ cup packed fresh parsley

½ cup packed fresh cilantro

¼ cup fresh dill, marjoram, mint, or thyme (or a combination)

1 garlic clove, minced

2 tablespoons olive oil

1 lemon, juiced

Up to 1 tablespoon water

ADD the farro, broth, canola oil, and a big pinch of salt to your Instant Pot. Secure the lid.

COOK at high pressure for 10 minutes and use a natural release. Drain well.

COMBINE the basil, parsley, cilantro, other herbs, and garlic in a blender or small food processor. Add the olive oil, lemon juice, and a pinch of salt. Pulse until pureed, adding up to 1 tablespoon water if needed.

TOSS the cooked farro with the pesto and taste for seasoning. Serve.

Israeli Couscous Salad

Israeli couscous, also known as pearl couscous, is like couscous hit with a grow ray. The dried pearls are about the size of whole peppercorns, and have a pleasantly chewy texture. They make a nice base for a pasta salad of sorts, with crunchy cucumbers, juicy tomatoes, tart pickled red onions, and fresh dill. Make this dish ahead of time for a barbecue or picnic lunch.

SERVES 4

3 cups water

½ red onion, thinly sliced

⅔ cup rice vinegar or apple cider vinegar

Salt

1 pinch sugar

2 tablespoons olive oil

1½ cups dried pearl (Israeli) couscous

2 garlic cloves, minced

1½ cups vegetable or chicken broth

3 to 4 Persian cucumbers, sliced (about 2 heaping cups)

10 ounces grape tomatoes, halved

2 heaping tablespoons chopped fresh dill

1 lemon, juiced

Pepper

BOIL the water. Place the onion in a fine-mesh strainer and slowly pour the hot water over the onion. Drain. Add the vinegar, a healthy pinch of salt, and a pinch of sugar to a Mason jar or other lidded container. Add the drained onion and shake well. Let sit, shaking occasionally, for 20 to 30 minutes.

MEANWHILE, turn on the Sauté function. Once hot, add 1 tablespoon oil. Add the couscous and garlic and cook, stirring, for about 3 minutes, until lightly toasted. Add the broth and a big pinch of salt. Turn off the Sauté function. Secure the lid.

COOK at high pressure for 5 minutes and use a quick release.

FLUFF the couscous with a fork and let cool for 5 to 10 minutes. Drain the pickled onion.

ADD 1 tablespoon oil, the pickled onion, cucumber, tomatoes, dill, and lemon juice to the couscous. Season with salt and pepper. Toss well and serve.

Boston Brown Bread

If you're not from New England, then it's unlikely you've come into contact with this canned bread. Yes, I said canned bread. Boston Brown Bread is a densely moist, lightly sweet, and flavorful quick bread that is traditionally cooked in (you guessed it) a can. The homemade version is a robust combination of rye flour, cornmeal, and molasses. Use blackstrap molasses for a deeply brown, bittersweet bread, or a less intense molasses for a less intense bread. Toast any leftovers and serve with butter or top with cheddar cheese.   SERVES 4 TO 6

Cooking spray

½ cup cornmeal

½ cup rye flour

½ cup whole wheat flour

1 tablespoon brown sugar

¾ teaspoon baking soda

½ teaspoon ground allspice

½ teaspoon salt

1 cup buttermilk, or ½ cup plain yogurt and ½ cup milk

⅓ cup molasses

⅓ cup raisins (optional)

CLEAN and completely dry two (14.5- or 15-ounce) empty cans (not pull-top). Grease the inside of each can well with cooking spray.

IN a medium mixing bowl, combine the cornmeal, rye flour, whole wheat flour, brown sugar, baking soda, allspice, and salt. Mix well. Add the buttermilk and molasses and mix just until totally combined. Fold in the raisins (if using).

FILL each can up two-thirds of the way and tap on the counter to release any air bubbles. Cover each tightly with aluminum foil.

ADD the trivet to your Instant Pot and place the cans on the trivet. Fill the pot with warm water about one-third of the way up the cans. Secure the lid.

COOK at high pressure for 20 minutes and use a natural release.

CAREFULLY remove the cans (they will be hot) and remove the aluminum foil. Test with a skewer or cake tester—if it comes out clean or with a few moist crumbs, the bread is done. If the inside is still wet, return to pressure for 3 more minutes and test again.

SLIDE the bread out of the can and let cool on a rack for a few minutes. Slice and serve warm with butter.

Creamy Cauliflower and White Cheddar Rotini

Did you know you can make a creamy bechamel-like sauce from cauliflower? Trust me on this! Instead of loading up your pasta with tons of cheese and cream, try adding some nutrition without sacrificing texture. And using sharp cheddar means you'll still get lots of cheesy flavor from just one cup of cheese.

SERVES 4 TO 6

2 tablespoons butter

4 garlic cloves, smashed

4 cups cauliflower florets (1 head)

3 cups vegetable broth or water (or a combination)

Salt and pepper

1 pound dried rotini pasta (regular, whole wheat, or veggie)

¼ cup milk or nondairy milk (soy, almond, or coconut)

½ lemon, juiced

1 cup shredded sharp white cheddar cheese

PUT a large pot of salted water on to boil.

TURN on the Sauté function. Once hot, add the butter and let melt. Add the garlic and cook for 30 seconds, or until fragrant. Flip the garlic and turn off the Sauté function. Add the cauliflower and broth and season with salt and pepper. Secure the lid.

COOK at high pressure for 4 minutes and use a quick release.

MEANWHILE, cook the rotini according to the package directions. Drain well.

ONCE the pressure has released, drain the cauliflower and garlic and reserve the cooking liquid. If you are using a blender, add the veggies, ½ cup of the cooking liquid, the milk, and lemon juice. Blend, with the lid cracked, until smooth. Alternatively, add all of the same ingredients to a small mixing bowl and blend using an immersion blender.

ADD up to ½ cup more cooking liquid to achieve desired consistency. The sauce should look like a thick alfredo sauce or a runny potato soup. Add the cheese and stir until melted. Taste for seasoning.

TOSS the cooked rotini with the sauce and serve.

P.S. Add cooked broccoli or peas to bulk this dish up, and serve it with a salad or chicken for a complete meal.

Giant White Beans and Romesco

Gigante, or giant Greek beans, are exactly as advertised. They're BIG, and they have the loveliest creamy texture. Even with their considerable size, they cook for just 20 minutes thanks to a presoak and a little pressure. The big beans can be found in Greek markets or ordered online. If you have trouble finding them (although they are worth seeking out), substitute cannellini beans and reduce the cook time to 8 minutes. SERVES 8

I pound dried gigante/giant Greek/giant white beans, presoaked and drained (see page 9)

4 cups water

3 cups vegetable or chicken broth

3 garlic cloves, smashed, plus I garlic clove, minced

I bay leaf

I teaspoon salt, plus more for seasoning

I red bell pepper

⅓ cup toasted slivered or blanched almonds

I tablespoon chopped fresh parsley

I teaspoon smoked or sweet paprika

½ teaspoon red pepper flakes

⅓ cup diced or crushed tomatoes, drained

I tablespoon sherry or red wine vinegar

¼ cup olive oil

Pepper

ADD presoaked beans, water, broth, smashed garlic, bay leaf, and salt to your Instant Pot. Secure the lid.

COOK at high pressure for 20 minutes and use a natural release. Taste a few different beans to see if they are cooked through. The beans should be creamy, not crunchy. If not completely cooked, cook for 3 to 5 more minutes at high pressure.

MEANWHILE, make the romesco: Preheat your broiler on high. Broil the bell pepper for 2 to 3 minutes, until charred, and turn. Repeat until all sides are well charred. Cover with aluminum foil and let sit for at least 10 minutes. Once cool, peel, stem, and seed the pepper. Roughly chop.

ADD the almonds, parsley, paprika, pepper flakes, and minced garlic to your food processor or blender. Pulse a few times, scraping down the sides as needed.

ADD the roasted pepper, the tomatoes, and vinegar. Blend. Add the oil in a stream while blending or pulsing. Season with salt and pepper.

DRAIN the cooked beans and discard the bay leaf. Top each serving with a large dollop of romesco.

Sticky Rice

Sticky Rice is made using a special kind of rice known by a few names: sweet, glutinous, and sticky. It's available in long-grain and short-grain varieties, and when steamed, turns into chewy, gluey rice that is really fun to eat. The side dish goes well with grilled chicken and papaya salad or Chinese sausage, or can simply stand in for white rice. SERVES 2 TO 4

1 cup long-grain sweet/glutinous/sticky Thai rice

3½ cups water

¼ teaspoon salt

PUT the rice, 2 cups water, and the salt in a small mixing bowl and stir. Let soak overnight or at least 1 hour. Drain well.

ADD 1½ cups water to the Instant Pot and add a steamer basket. Line the basket with cheesecloth and add the drained rice on top of the cheesecloth, spreading it out on top of the basket. Let the cheesecloth loosely overlap on top of the rice. Secure the lid.

COOK at high pressure for 12 minutes and use a natural release for 5 minutes followed by a quick release.

CAREFULLY dump the rice into a serving bowl, peeling it off the cheesecloth, and serve immediately.

P.S. All Instant Potters should own cheesecloth. In addition to this recipe, you can use it to strain your homemade yogurt, turning it into creamy Greek yogurt. A clean, thin piece of white cotton fabric (such as a handkerchief) will work in a pinch.

Chinese Five-Spice Black-Eyed Peas

Five-spice powder is a mix of clove, star anise, peppercorns, fennel, and cassia, and is used in many Chinese dishes. It's easy to find in any Asian market or in the international section of your grocery store. Lightly sweet and spicy, it adds something special to black-eyed peas. Vinegar lends a savory, sour note and sriracha gives everything a bit of heat for a top-notch side dish.

SERVES 4 OR 5

8 ounces dried black-eyed peas, presoaked and drained (see page 9)

½ onion, halved

2 garlic cloves, smashed, plus 2 garlic cloves, minced

1 bay leaf

3 teaspoons canola or grapeseed oil

½ teaspoon salt, plus more for seasoning

4 cups water

1½ teaspoons Chinese five-spice powder

1 tablespoon rice wine vinegar

2 to 3 teaspoons sriracha

Pepper

ADD the presoaked black-eyed peas, onion, smashed garlic, bay leaf, 1 teaspoon oil, the salt, and water to your Instant Pot. Secure the lid.

COOK at high pressure for 5 minutes and use a natural release.

WHILE the pressure is releasing, add 2 teaspoons oil to a small skillet over medium heat. Once hot, add the minced garlic and sauté for 30 seconds. Add the Chinese five-spice and stir, then remove from the heat. Add the vinegar and sriracha and stir.

ONCE the pressure has released, taste to see if the black-eyed peas are cooked through. If they are not quite soft enough, return to pressure for 2 minutes until cooked. Discard the onion, garlic, and bay leaf. Drain the beans and return to the pot.

DRIZZLE with the five-spice and vinegar mixture. Season with salt and pepper and gently toss. Serve.

Quinoa Salad with Edamame and Corn

Quinoa, a super-duper food, only needs a minute of pressure and a natural release to perfectly steam. White, red, or tri-color quinoa will work equally well. Tossed together with edamame, corn, arugula, cotija cheese, and pepitas, the salad covers lots of nutritional bases and a superb range of flavors and textures. Eat as is for lunch, or serve as a side with fish or chicken.

SERVES 5 TO 6

1 cup red or white quinoa, rinsed and drained

1½ cups water

1 teaspoon plus 2 tablespoons canola or grapeseed oil

½ teaspoon salt, plus more for seasoning

1 lemon, juiced

1 teaspoon fresh thyme leaves

1 teaspoon ground cumin

½ teaspoon honey

Pepper

1 cup fresh or frozen shelled edamame

1 cup fresh or frozen corn kernels

3 cups packed arugula

½ cup crumbled cotija cheese or mild, firm feta cheese

¼ cup toasted pepitas (pumpkin seeds)

ADD the quinoa, water, 1 teaspoon oil, and salt to your Instant Pot. Secure the lid.

COOK at high pressure for 1 minute and use a natural release.

MEANWHILE, make the dressing: Combine the lemon juice, thyme, cumin, and honey and season with salt and pepper. Gradually add 2 tablespoons oil while whisking.

ONCE the pressure has released, add the edamame and corn to the pot and stir. Let the mixture cool to room temperature or place in the refrigerator to chill.

ONCE cooled, add the arugula, cotija cheese, and dressing and toss well. Taste for seasoning. Serve topped with pepitas.

Barley and Sugar Snap Pea Salad

Chewy barley and snappy snap peas are a match made in salad heaven. Radishes add a little peppery crunch, and it's all cooled off by salty feta and fresh mint. Make the barley ahead of time, or make the whole thing ahead of time. Serve cold or at room temperature. SERVES 4

I cup pearled barley

3 cups vegetable broth or water (or a combination)

I teaspoon canola or grapeseed oil

½ teaspoon salt plus more for seasoning

I large lime, juiced

I teaspoon honey

½ teaspoon chili powder

Pepper

2 tablespoons olive oil

8 ounces sugar snap peas, chopped (1½ cups)

I cup sliced radishes (I small bunch)

½ cup toasted almonds

½ cup crumbled feta cheese

¼ cup chopped fresh mint

COMBINE the barley, broth, canola oil, and salt in your Instant Pot. Secure the lid.

COOK at high pressure for 18 minutes and use a natural release for 10 minutes followed by a quick release.

DRAIN the barley and rinse well with cold water. While the barley is draining and cooling off, make the dressing: In a small bowl, combine the lime juice, honey, and chili powder, and season with salt and pepper. Add the olive oil while whisking.

COMBINE the cooled barley, sugar snap peas, radishes, almonds, feta, and mint in a large bowl and toss. Top with the dressing and toss well to coat. Taste for seasoning and serve.

P.S. If you can get your hands on chewier, healthier hulled barley, it's even better. Cook it for 30 minutes instead of 18.

Bleu Cheese and Caramelized Onion Polenta

I can think of no better side dish for grilled steak than Bleu Cheese and Caramelized Onion Polenta. Funky cheese and sweet caramelized onions elevate creamy polenta, and the dish is perfection sitting under a pile of sliced steak or chicken. Use your bleu cheese of choice as long as it's not too firm.

SERVES 4

4 cups vegetable or chicken broth

1 teaspoon plus 1 tablespoon olive oil

1 teaspoon salt, plus more for seasoning

1 cup dried polenta

1 large onion, sliced

1 pinch sugar

1 tablespoon butter

¼ cup heavy cream, or 3 tablespoons whole milk

2 ounces bleu cheese, crumbled

TURN on the Sauté function. Add the broth, 1 teaspoon oil, and the salt and bring to a simmer. While constantly whisking, add the polenta slowly. Quickly secure the lid and turn off the Sauté function.

COOK at high pressure for 8 minutes and use a natural release for 10 minutes followed by a controlled quick release.

MEANWHILE, heat a large skillet over medium-high heat. Once hot, add the onion and cook, stirring occasionally, for about 5 minutes, or until browned but not burnt.

ADD 1 tablespoon oil, a pinch of salt, and the sugar and stir. Sauté until tender and caramelized, 5 to 10 minutes.

ONCE the pressure has released, add the butter and cream to the polenta and whisk vigorously until smooth. Add half of the bleu cheese and mix. Top with the onion and remaining cheese and serve immediately.

P.S. All of the recipes in this book are best if you turn off the Keep Warm function, but it's especially important for this dish to avoid scorching.

Boiled Peanuts

If you're not from a peanut-growing region, there's a chance you've never experienced boiled peanuts. More commonly roasted, raw peanuts can also be boiled for hours with salt for a totally different effect. The nuts get a little soft, kind of buttery, and lightly salty. It might not be the snack you're used to, but boiled peanuts are incredibly addictive. Pressure cooking shrinks the cook time down to a hands-off hour or two. SERVES 6

1 pound raw, in-shell peanuts

¼ cup salt

Water

OPTIONAL FLAVORINGS (CHOOSE ONE):

1 tablespoon barbecue seasoning

1 tablespoon Cajun seasoning

RINSE the peanuts well and drain. Add to your Instant Pot along with the salt. Add enough water so that when you press down on the floating peanuts they are covered by about 1 inch of water. Add a seasoning if desired. Put a steamer basket or trivet on top to keep the peanuts submerged. Secure the lid.

COOK at high pressure for 1 hour and use a natural release.

TASTE a peanut to see if they are done to your liking. If they are too hard, return to pressure for up to 1 additional hour. The cook time will depend upon how fresh your peanuts are and how you like them.

DRAIN the peanuts. Serve warm. Store leftovers in the fridge.

Veggie Sides

Spaghetti Squash with Mushrooms and Pancetta

Ghee Mashed Potatoes

Glazed Beets with Chive Sour Cream

Sesame and Garlic Whole Carrots

Creamed Collard Greens

Stewed Kale with White Wine and Breadcrumbs

Braised Cabbage, Fennel, and Apples

Red Potatoes and Green Beans with Herb Aioli

Mashed Plantains

Eggplant and Goat Cheese Crostini

Butternut Squash and Sweet Potato Mash

Stewed Parsnips and Carrots

Braised Artichoke with Tahini Sauce

Spaghetti Squash with Mushrooms and Pancetta

Spaghetti squash is a magical vegetable that starts out as a hard, unassuming squash and turns into toothsome yellow spaghetti. Steaming is the best method for making this transformation, and a quick trip in the Instant Pot does the trick. Crispy pancetta, savory mushrooms, and salty parmesan are a simple but full-flavored topping for a low-carb dish. SERVES 4 OR 5

1 (2-pound) spaghetti squash

1 cup water

2 tablespoons olive oil

2 ounces pancetta, finely chopped

8 ounces cremini mushrooms, sliced

2 garlic cloves, minced

1 teaspoon finely chopped fresh sage leaves (optional)

Salt and pepper

¼ cup grated parmesan cheese

CUT the spaghetti squash through the middle rather than longways, creating two circles instead of two ovals. Use a spoon to scoop out all of the pulp and seeds.

ADD the trivet to your Instant Pot and add the water. Place the squash cut side up on the trivet. Secure the lid.

COOK at high pressure for 8 minutes and use a quick release.

MEANWHILE, heat a medium skillet over medium heat. Once hot, add 1 tablespoon oil and the pancetta. Cook for about 1 minute, until starting to crisp up. Add the mushrooms and garlic and sauté for 4 to 5 minutes, until the pancetta is crisp and the mushrooms are tender and browned. Add the sage (if using) and season with salt and pepper. Set aside.

ONCE the pressure has released, carefully remove the hot squash and dump out any water. Let cool for a few minutes until safe to handle. Run a fork around the inside of the squash, following the circle, to release the strands. Continue scraping the squash until all of the meat is free and dump into a bowl.

DRIZZLE the squash strands with 1 tablespoon oil and season with salt and pepper. Toss. Serve topped with the mushrooms and pancetta followed by the parmesan.

Ghee Mashed Potatoes

Ghee is a type of clarified butter that's frequently used in Indian cuisine. It's pure butterfat that's lightly toasted, lending a mild buttery flavor to your mashed potatoes. Ghee is also great for sautéing and high-heat cooking, since its smoke point is much higher than that of regular butter. Add richness to the dish by throwing in a bit of sour cream, or swapping out the milk for buttermilk.

SERVES 4 OR 5

2 pounds Yukon Gold or white potatoes, peeled and cut into 1-inch chunks

3 garlic cloves, smashed

3 cups water

¼ cup to ½ cup whole milk

¼ cup ghee

Salt and pepper

ADD the potatoes, garlic, and water to your Instant Pot. Secure the lid.

COOK at high pressure for 8 minutes and use a quick release.

DRAIN the potatoes and garlic and return to the pot. Add ¼ cup milk and all of the ghee. Mash until smooth, adding more milk if needed. Season with salt and pepper to taste and serve.

P.S. If you can't find ghee at your grocery store or want to save some cash by making your own, here's how you do it: Melt a stick of butter over medium-low heat. Let cook until the butter smells toasty and some of the solids at the bottom have begun to brown but not burn, 7 to 10 minutes. Turn off the heat and tilt the pan to one side. Use a spoon to skim off all of the whey foam at the top. Strain through a piece of cheesecloth and refrigerate until ready to use.

Glazed Beets with Chive Sour Cream

Beets are effortless in the pressure cooker, steaming to perfection with very little mess. Cooking them whole makes them easy to peel, and a sauté in honey and balsamic vinegar gives them a nice glaze. Serve with the chive sour cream on the side for dipping. SERVES 3 OR 4

1 pound small or medium beets, trimmed

1 cup water

⅓ cup sour cream

1 tablespoon finely chopped fresh chives

Salt and pepper

2 teaspoons butter

2 teaspoons honey

1 teaspoon balsamic vinegar

ADD the beets and water to your Instant Pot. Secure the lid.

COOK at high pressure for 13 minutes for small beets and 18 minutes for medium beets. Use a quick release. Test for doneness using a sharp knife.

MEANWHILE, in a small bowl combine the sour cream and chives and season with salt and pepper.

CAREFULLY drain the beets and run them under cold water. Once they are cool enough to handle, peel the beets and quarter them. Wipe out the pot.

TURN on the Sauté function. Once hot, add the butter and let melt. Add the honey and vinegar followed by the beets. Sauté for 2 minutes, or until well coated. Turn off the Sauté function. Season with salt and pepper. Serve with chive sour cream.

Sesame and Garlic Whole Carrots

Hearty carrots can stand up to the quiet intensity of pressure cooking, especially when they're left whole. The Instant Pot can simulate a quick braise, and after a few short minutes the carrots turn out creamy but not mushy. Rainbow carrots are especially lovely in this dish if you can find them. Try pairing these beauties with Chicken and Olive Tagine (page 33).

SERVES 4

1 tablespoon butter

1 pound medium whole rainbow or regular carrots, trimmed (make sure they'll fit lying flat in your pressure cooker)

1 cup water

2 teaspoons sesame oil

2 garlic cloves, minced

Salt

1 teaspoon sesame seeds

TURN on the Sauté function. Once hot, add the butter and let melt. Add the carrots and cook for 1 minute, tossing a few times. Turn off the Sauté function. Add the water and secure the lid.

COOK at high pressure for 2 minutes and use a quick release.

DRAIN the carrots and wipe out the pot. Return the pot to the cooker and turn on the Sauté function. Once hot, add the sesame oil and garlic and sauté for 1 minute, or until lightly browned.

TURN off the Sauté function and add the carrots. Toss and season with salt. Serve topped with sesame seeds.

P.S. This recipe is easy to customize. Instead of garlic and sesame, try tossing the carrots with soy sauce and honey or red pepper flakes and lemon juice. Or just add a dollop of fresh pesto.

Creamed Collard Greens

Move over, spinach, collard greens can take it from here. Even if you're not sure that you like collard greens, just do me a favor and try Creamed Collard Greens. After the greens are stewed with garlic, they meet up with a cream sauce and a little parmesan cheese for a dish that's just decadent enough. It's the world's best side for chicken or steak, and plays nice with potato or bean sides, too.

SERVES 4 OR 5

1 tablespoon olive oil

½ onion, diced

3 garlic cloves, sliced

2 pounds collard greens, thick stems removed and leaves chopped

1 cup vegetable broth

3 tablespoons butter

1 tablespoon all-purpose flour

¾ cup heavy cream

¼ cup grated parmesan cheese

1 pinch grated nutmeg

Salt and pepper

TURN on the Sauté function. Once hot, add the oil followed by the onion. Sauté for 2 minutes and add the garlic. Stir and turn off the Sauté function. Add the collard greens and broth. Secure the lid.

COOK at high pressure for 20 minutes and use a quick release.

DRAIN the collard greens, onions, and garlic. Set aside. Clean out the pot, dry, and return to the cooker.

TURN on the Sauté function. Once hot, add the butter and let melt. Add the flour and stir until combined. Add the cream and cook, stirring, until the mixture is vigorously boiling and starts to thicken. Turn off the Sauté function.

ADD the collard greens mixture, parmesan, and nutmeg. Season with salt and pepper and stir. Serve warm.

P.S. Collard greens can be pretty dirty. Fill your sink with cool water and dunk the leaves, then let them soak for about 20 minutes. The dirt should sink to the bottom.

Stewed Kale with White Wine and Breadcrumbs

Collards aren't the only green that likes being stewed—kale turns buttery without falling apart after a quick stint in the Instant Pot. White wine and broth add complexity, and a topping of crispy, garlicky breadcrumbs gives the side dish some texture. SERVES 4

2 tablespoons olive oil

2 garlic cloves, sliced, plus 1 garlic clove, finely minced

¼ cup dry white wine

1 cup vegetable broth

2 bunches lacinato kale (aka dinosaur, Tuscan, or black kale), tough ends removed and leaves chopped

¼ cup panko breadcrumbs

¼ teaspoon red pepper flakes

Salt and pepper

TURN on the Sauté function. Once hot, add 1 tablespoon oil followed by the sliced garlic. Sauté for 30 seconds and add the wine. Cook for about 3 minutes, until the wine has reduced by half. Turn off the Sauté function. Add the broth and kale. Secure the lid.

COOK for 5 minutes at high pressure and use a quick release.

MEANWHILE, heat 1 tablespoon oil in a small skillet over medium heat. Add the minced garlic and cook for 30 seconds. Add the breadcrumbs and pepper flakes and stir. Season with salt and pepper. Cook, stirring, for about 3 minutes, until the breadcrumbs are toasted. Remove from the heat.

ONCE the pressure has released, drain the kale and garlic. Season with salt and pepper and top with the breadcrumbs. Serve.

Braised Cabbage, Fennel, and Apples

Purple cabbage, fresh fennel, and apple gently cook down and become a brightly hued, buttery dish that's excellent served alongside sausage. A touch of vinegar and lemon keep things bright, and the dish can be served hot, cold, or at room temperature. SERVES 4 OR 5

2 tablespoons butter

½ onion, sliced

1 large apple, peeled, cored, and chopped

½ small head red cabbage, cored and chopped

1 large bulb fennel, fronds and tough base removed, bulb roughly chopped, and 1 tablespoon chopped fronds reserved for garnish

½ cup vegetable or chicken broth

2 teaspoons apple cider vinegar

1 teaspoon honey

1 squeeze fresh lemon juice

Salt and pepper

TURN on the Sauté function. Once hot, add 1 tablespoon butter and melt. Add the onion and cook for 2 minutes. Add the apple and sauté for 1 more minute. Turn off the Sauté function. Add the cabbage, fennel, and broth. Secure the lid.

COOK at high pressure for 5 minutes and use a quick release.

DRAIN off most of the cooking liquid. Add 1 tablespoon butter, the vinegar, honey, and lemon juice. Season with salt and pepper and toss. Garnish with fennel fronds and serve.

P.S. This recipe also works with green or savoy cabbage, but it won't have that bright purple hue.

Red Potatoes and Green Beans with Herb Aioli

When I was growing up, more often than not my family meals included a side dish of red potatoes and green beans. My grandmother's recipe included bacon or ham hock, but for this vegetarian version I drizzle the perfectly tender veggies with a homemade parsley aioli. Aioli is easier to make than you'd think—just add the oil slowly and whisk, whisk, whisk.

SERVES 4

1 pound small red potatoes, halved

1½ to 2 cups vegetable or chicken broth

1 pound fresh green beans, trimmed (thick green beans work best)

1 large egg yolk

2 teaspoons fresh lemon juice

¼ teaspoon Dijon mustard

¼ cup olive oil

2 tablespoons canola or grapeseed oil

1 garlic clove, finely grated

1 tablespoon finely chopped fresh parsley

Salt and pepper

2 teaspoons water

ADD the potatoes to your Instant Pot and enough broth to mostly cover. Top with the green beans. Secure the lid.

COOK at high pressure for 4 minutes and use a quick release.

MEANWHILE, make the aioli: In a small mixing bowl, combine the egg yolk, lemon juice, and mustard and whisk. Very slowly add the olive oil followed by the canola oil, whisking vigorously the whole time. If the mixture starts to separate, stop adding oil and whisk until smooth, then continue.

ADD the garlic and parsley and season with salt and pepper. Whisk. Add the water and whisk until smooth.

ONCE the pressure has released, drain the potatoes and beans completely. Season with salt and pepper. Serve drizzled with the aioli.

Mashed Plantains

Known in different cultures as mofongo, fufu, and mangú (among other names), mashed plantains are a staple of many cuisines. Sautéed onion and garlic are added for flavor and texture, and you can add some chopped crispy bacon if you really want to. Though usually made with green plantains, I've included instructions for using green or yellow. The yellow version is sweeter and is great with spicy black beans; the green version is a superb pair for anything pork.   SERVES 3 OR 4

2 large green or yellow plantains

2 garlic cloves, smashed, plus 1 garlic clove, minced

1 cup vegetable or chicken broth

1 tablespoon olive oil

½ small onion, finely diced

1 tablespoon butter

Salt and pepper

PREPARE your plantains: If you are using green (unripe) plantains, they can be tricky to peel. Cut the plantain in half longways and in half again around the middle. Use your fingers to pry off the peel, using a paring knife to remove any remaining pieces. If you are using yellow (ripe) plantains, they are almost as easy to peel as a banana. Cut in half once longways and peel. For both types: cut or scrape out most of the seeds and the tough center.

ADD the peeled and cut plantains, smashed garlic cloves, and broth to your Instant Pot. Secure the lid.

COOK at high pressure for 5 minutes for yellow plantains and 7 minutes for green plantains. Use a quick release.

MEANWHILE, heat a small skillet over medium heat. Add the oil followed by the onion. Sauté for 3 minutes and add the minced garlic. Sauté for 2 to 3 more minutes, until the onion is translucent.

ONCE the pressure has released, drain the plantains and garlic, reserving the cooking liquid. Add them back to the pot along with the butter and ¼ cup of the cooking liquid. Mash well and add more liquid as needed to achieve the desired consistency. Note that the mash will thicken up as it sits, so if you are not serving it immediately, keep the rest of the cooking liquid handy to mix in as needed.

ADD the sautéed onion and garlic and season generously with salt and pepper. Serve.

Eggplant and Goat Cheese Crostini

Eggplant and Goat Cheese Crostini are perfect party food. They only take a few minutes to prepare, look fancy, are veggie-friendly, and can be served at room temperature. Sometimes I make them for dinner and eat them while I watch Netflix by myself (party of one). The eggplant gains smoky flavor from being charred in the pot before pressure cooking transforms it into a silky spread. Goat cheese adds a good tang and the basil gives the app a little fresh spice.

SERVES 6

1 tablespoon canola or grapeseed oil

1 (1-pound) eggplant, top removed, mostly peeled and cut in half longways

4 garlic cloves, smashed

1 cup vegetable broth

1 baguette, cut into thin slices

2 tablespoons olive oil

3 ounces soft goat cheese

½ lemon, zested and juiced

½ teaspoon red pepper flakes

Salt and pepper

2 tablespoons fresh basil leaves

TURN on the Sauté function to high. Once hot, add the canola oil. Add the eggplant cut side down and let cook for about 5 minutes, or until charred but not burnt. Add the garlic and turn off the Sauté function. Add the broth. Secure the lid.

COOK at high pressure for 10 minutes and use a quick release.

MEANWHILE, preheat your broiler. Drizzle the slices of baguette with olive oil on both sides. Toast, turning once, until lightly crispy. Let cool for a few minutes and spread each slice with goat cheese.

DRAIN the eggplant well and return to the pot, discarding the cooking liquid. Add the lemon zest and juice and pepper flakes, and season with salt and pepper. Mix and mash well.

TO serve, top each slice of baguette with the eggplant mash and garnish with basil.

Butternut Squash and Sweet Potato Mash

Mashed potatoes are awesome, but they aren't the be-all and end-all of mashed side dishes. For a different flavor with a similar texture, try lightly sweet butternut squash and sweet potatoes. All you need to add is a little butter and maple syrup to make a dish that's surprisingly just as savory as it is sweet. Serve with steak or chicken and tender-crisp green beans.

SERVES 3 OR 4

1 pound butternut squash, peeled and cut into 1-inch chunks

1 pound sweet potato, peeled and cut into 1-inch chunks

1½ cups vegetable or chicken broth

1½ cups water

2 tablespoons butter, cubed

1 teaspoon maple syrup

1 pinch grated nutmeg

Salt and pepper

ADD the butternut squash and sweet potato to your Instant Pot. Add the broth and water (just enough to cover almost all of the veggies) and secure the lid.

COOK at high pressure for 5 minutes and use a natural release for 10 minutes followed by a quick release.

DRAIN and save the cooking liquid for soup. Return the squash and sweet potato to the pot. Add the butter, maple syrup, and nutmeg. Season with salt and pepper. Mash well until smooth and mixed. Serve warm.

Stewed Parsnips and Carrots

Parsnips and carrots turn creamy and lightly sweet after just a few minutes in the Instant Pot, and they make an excellent side dish for red meat (like Braised Short Ribs with Mushrooms, page 54). Cut them into chunks 1 to 1½ inches long depending on the diameter (longer chunks when chopping the skinny sections, shorter when chopping the thick ends).

SERVES 2 OR 3

8 ounces carrots, peeled and cut into 1-inch chunks

8 ounces parsnips, peeled and cut into 1-inch chunks

1 cup vegetable or chicken broth

1 tablespoon butter

1 teaspoon fresh thyme leaves

1 teaspoon fresh lemon juice

Salt and pepper

ADD the carrots, parsnips, and broth to your Instant Pot. Secure the lid.

COOK at high pressure for 2 minutes and use a natural release.

DRAIN the carrots and parsnips, reserving the cooking liquid for soup or another recipe that calls for vegetable broth. Add the butter, thyme, and lemon juice to the veggies and season with salt and pepper. Serve.

P.S. This recipe is good for doubling. You may not need a full 2 cups broth—just enough to cover three-quarters of the veggies.

Braised Artichoke with Tahini Sauce

Fresh artichokes can be intimidating. They take a lot of prep work, and if you don't prepare them right, you could end up with a pretty unpleasant experience. Using Mark Bittman's braising method, there's relatively little work and the results are delightful every time. Eat the leaves one at a time, grabbing each one by the pointy end and using your teeth to scrape out all of the tender meat. The heart and inner stem can be eaten in their entirety—just don't forget the lemony, garlicky tahini sauce.   SERVES 2

1 medium to large globe artichoke	⅓ cup tahini
1 lemon, cut into quarters	1 garlic clove, finely grated
2 tablespoons butter	Salt and pepper
1 cup chicken or vegetable broth	¼ to ⅓ cup water

TURN on the Sauté function.

PREPARE the artichoke: Cut off at least 1 inch of the stem. Remove the outermost, hardest leaves and trim off the nubs they leave behind with a paring knife. Cut the artichoke in half, top to bottom, and rub both sides with one lemon quarter. Use a spoon (a grapefruit spoon works great here) to remove all of the feathery bits in the middle called the choke and the innermost prickly leaves. Rub with lemon and repeat with the other half.

ADD the butter to the pot and let melt. Add both halves of the artichoke in a single layer, cut side down. Let cook, without moving, for 5 minutes, or until browned. Turn off the Sauté function. Add the broth and secure the lid.

COOK at high pressure for 5 minutes for a medium artichoke and 6 minutes for a large artichoke. Use a natural release.

MEANWHILE, make the tahini sauce: Combine the tahini and garlic and season with salt and pepper. Use the juice from the remaining lemon wedges and mix—the mixture will become stiff. Whisk in ¼ cup warm water until the mixture is the consistency of yogurt. Use more water if needed.

SERVE the artichokes with the tahini dipping sauce.

Soups and Stews

Creamy Lots of Mushrooms Soup

Garbure (Ham and White Bean Stew)

Black Lentil Soup with Bacon and Chard

Smoky Shrimp Pozole

Root Vegetable Soup with Garlic Croutons

Chicken Paprikash Stew

Turkey Black Bean Chili

Green Tortilla Soup

Preserved Lemon and Garlic Lamb Stew

Chicken and Split Pea Soup

Creamy Spinach and Potato Soup

Vegetarian Gumbo

Cheater Ramen (Japanese Chicken Noodle Soup)

Beer and Bean Chili

Curried Cauliflower and Butternut Squash Soup

Spicy Chicken Sausage Pasta e Fagioli

Creamy Lots of Mushrooms Soup

Are you really into mushrooms? If the answer is yes, then keep reading. If the answer is no, then kindly skip to the next recipe and share this one with a mushroom-loving friend. Inspired by a forgivingly simple Jamie Oliver dish, Creamy Lots of Mushrooms Soup combines all sorts of mushrooms (even dried ones) with fresh thyme and a little heavy cream for a deeply flavored and luxurious soup. Serve with grilled or toasted bread. SERVES 4

5 to 6 dried shiitake mushrooms, broken up

2 cups boiling water

2 tablespoons butter

I small onion, diced

4 garlic cloves, smashed

½ cup dry white wine

I teaspoon fresh thyme leaves

I pound mixed fresh mushrooms, such as cremini, oyster, shiitake, and button, sliced

Salt and pepper

2½ to 3 cups plus 2 tablespoons chicken or vegetable broth

2 teaspoons olive oil

¼ cup heavy cream

I tablespoon fresh lemon juice

2 teaspoons soy sauce

I tablespoon chopped fresh parsley (optional)

Truffle oil, for serving (optional)

PUT the dried mushrooms in a small bowl and pour boiling hot water over them. Let them sit until it's time to add them to the Instant Pot.

TURN on the Sauté function. Once hot, add the butter and let melt. Add the onion and sauté for 3 minutes. Add the garlic and sauté for 1 minute. Drain and add the dried mushrooms, followed by the wine and thyme. Let the mixture simmer for about 3 minutes, until the wine has mostly evaporated. Turn off the Sauté function.

ADD all but 2 cups of the sliced mushrooms and season with salt and pepper. Add 2½ cups broth. Secure the lid.

COOK at high pressure for 30 minutes and use a natural release.

MEANWHILE, heat the oil over medium heat in a medium skillet. Once hot, add the reserved mushrooms and sauté for 5 minutes. Add 2 tablespoons broth and cook until it has evaporated and the mushrooms are tender and a nice brown color. Season with salt and pepper and set aside.

ONCE the pressure has released, add the cream, lemon juice, and soy sauce to the pot and stir. Use an immersion blender to blend the soup, or let cool for a bit and puree

(continued)

in a blender with the lid cracked. Add up to ½ cup more broth to reach the desired consistency.

ADD the sautéed mushrooms and taste for seasoning. Serve topped with the parsley and small drizzle of truffle oil (if using).

Garbure (Ham and White Bean Stew)

Garbure is a French stew that combines whatever meat, vegetables, and beans are available into a filling one-bowl meal. Ham hock adds tons of smoky flavor without overtaking the soup, and tender potatoes and white beans make the dish creamy without a drop of dairy. Serve with crusty bread and a hunk of cheese.   SERVES 4 TO 6

1 tablespoon olive oil

1 small onion, diced

1 large carrot, diced

1 large celery rib, diced

4 garlic cloves, minced

1 pound smoked ham hock

5 cups chicken or vegetable broth

8 ounces dried cannellini beans, presoaked and drained (see page 9)

4 cups chopped savoy, green, or napa cabbage

1 pound red potatoes, cut into 1-inch chunks

4 fresh thyme sprigs

1 bay leaf

Salt and pepper

TURN on the Sauté function. Once hot, add the oil followed by the onion, carrot, celery, and garlic. Sauté for 3 minutes. Turn off the Sauté function. Add the ham hock and broth. Secure the lid.

COOK at high pressure for 40 minutes and use a controlled quick release.

ADD the beans, cabbage, potatoes, thyme, and bay leaf. Season with salt and pepper. Make sure all of the beans and potatoes are submerged. Secure the lid.

COOK at high pressure for 8 minutes and use a natural release.

REMOVE the bay leaf. Remove the ham hock and pick off any meat, adding it back to the soup and discarding the bone. Taste for seasoning, then serve.

Black Lentil Soup with Bacon and Chard

If you like your lentil soup like you like your dramas (dark and mysterious), take Black Lentil Soup with Bacon and Chard for a spin. Black lentils, also known as beluga lentils for their resemblance to caviar, make an ample base, and bacon adds smoky meatiness. Top with a dollop of sour cream or crème fraîche or eat it as is.

SERVES 3 OR 4

6 ounces bacon (2 to 3 slices, depending on thickness)

2 teaspoons olive oil

½ large onion, diced

3 to 4 large chard leaves, stems removed and chopped into ½-inch pieces, leaves chopped (about 3 cups loosely packed)

4 garlic cloves, minced

1½ teaspoons tomato paste

1 teaspoon fresh thyme leaves

1 cup beluga/black lentils, rinsed and picked over

3½ cups chicken broth

Salt and pepper

1 teaspoon sherry vinegar

PREHEAT a large skillet over medium heat. Add the bacon and cook, turning halfway through, until crisp. Reserve 2 teaspoons of the bacon fat. Once the bacon is cool enough to handle, chop into small pieces.

TURN on the Sauté function. Add the reserved bacon fat and the oil, followed by the onion and chard stems. Sauté for 3 minutes. Add the garlic and cook for 1 more minute, stirring. Turn off the Sauté function.

ADD the tomato paste and thyme and stir. Add the chard leaves, lentils, broth, and bacon, reserving some crispy pieces for garnish. Season with salt and pepper and stir. Secure the lid.

COOK at high pressure for 10 minutes and use a natural release.

TASTE to make sure the lentils are fully cooked and taste for seasoning. If the lentils are not quite done, cook for another 3 minutes at high pressure. Add the vinegar and stir. Garnish with crispy bacon and serve.

P.S. You can use green lentils for this recipe, but the results will be decidedly less brooding.

Smoky Shrimp Pozole

Pozole is a Mexican stew with lots of flavor and a few key ingredients: dried chiles, hominy (cooked dried corn kernels), and pork. My version is quicker and lighter thanks to replacing a big hunk of slow-cooking pork with smoky bacon and tender shrimp. You can find New Mexico chiles in a Mexican market or the international section of the grocery store. Rehydrated and blended, they add a not-too-spicy kick and a depth that you won't find with fresh chiles.

SERVES 4

4 dried New Mexico chiles (about 1.25 ounces)

4 garlic cloves, smashed, plus 4 garlic cloves, minced

1 cup water

4 slices bacon, roughly chopped

1 tablespoon canola or grapeseed oil

1 small onion, diced

1 small green bell pepper, diced

1 tablespoon tomato paste

1 teaspoon ground cumin

½ teaspoon dried oregano

2 cups chicken or vegetable broth

1 (25-ounce) can hominy, drained

Salt and pepper

8 ounces raw peeled shrimp

½ lime, juiced

PREPARE THE DRIED CHILES: Wearing gloves, cut the stems off the chiles and slice down the middle of each, scraping out as many seeds as you can. Add the chiles, smashed garlic cloves, and water to the Instant Pot. Secure the lid.

COOK at high pressure for 7 minutes and use a natural release. Pour the chile mixture into a blender and let cool. Clean out the pot, dry, and return to the cooker.

TURN on the Sauté function. Once hot, add the bacon and cook until lightly crispy. Remove the bacon and set aside. Add the oil to the pot followed by the onion. Sauté for 2 minutes. Add the bell pepper, minced garlic, and tomato paste and sauté for 2 more minutes. Add the cumin and oregano, stir, and turn off the Sauté function.

ADD the broth and scrape the bottom of the pot. Chop the cooked bacon and add it to the pot. Add the hominy and season with salt and pepper, then stir. Secure the lid.

COOK at high pressure for 5 minutes and use a natural release.

MEANWHILE, blend the peppers, garlic, and cooking liquid until smooth.

ONCE the pressure has released, add the blended chile mixture to the soup. Turn on the Sauté function. Once simmering, add the shrimp and cook for 1 minute. Turn off the Sauté function and add the lime juice. Loosely cover and let sit for 5 minutes, then serve.

P.S. Wearing gloves while you handle the chiles helps keep any chile oil from sinking into your palms and causing some real eye pain later. It's a nice idea to crack a window while cooking and blending the chiles too.

Root Vegetable Soup with Garlic Croutons

Root Vegetable Soup has autumn written all over it, but it's totally tasty any time of year. Sweet potatoes, parsnips, and carrots offer natural sweetness and a beautiful orange color. Ginger and cumin give the soup a bit of spice, and the whole thing is pureed into a creamy soup before being topped with crispy, garlicky croutons.

SERVES 5 OR 6

1 tablespoon olive oil

1 onion, diced

4 garlic cloves, smashed, plus 1 garlic clove, cut in half

1 pound sweet potatoes, peeled and chopped

1 pound parsnips, peeled and chopped

8 ounces carrots, peeled and chopped

8 ounces Yukon Gold or white potatoes, peeled and chopped

2 cups vegetable broth

1 (13.5-ounce) can coconut milk

6 ounces rustic bread, sliced into ½-inch slices (stale bread works best)

2 tablespoons butter, melted

Salt and pepper

2 teaspoons grated fresh ginger, or 1 teaspoon ground ginger

1 teaspoon ground cumin

1 teaspoon fresh thyme leaves, plus more for garnish

PREHEAT your oven to 375 degrees.

TURN on the Sauté function. Once hot, add the oil followed by the onion. Sauté for 2 minutes and add the smashed garlic. Sauté for 1 more minute and turn off the Sauté function. Add the sweet potatoes, parsnips, carrots, potatoes, broth, and coconut milk. Secure the lid.

COOK at high pressure for 10 minutes and use a natural release.

MEANWHILE, rub each slice of bread with the cut garlic. Cut into 1-inch cubes. Place the bread on a baking sheet and toss with the melted butter. Sprinkle with salt. Bake for 5 minutes, toss, and bake for 5 to 8 minutes more, depending on how stale your bread is, until toasty.

ONCE the pressure has released, add the ginger, cumin, and thyme to the pot, and season with salt and pepper. Blend the soup using an immersion blender or by pureeing in two batches in a blender with the lid cracked.

TASTE for seasoning. Serve topped with a sprinkle of fresh thyme and the garlic croutons.

Chicken Paprikash Stew

A traditional Hungarian dish, paprikash is an especially comforting dish with chicken, tomato, red pepper, sour cream, and a healthy dose of paprika. The paprika (smoked or sweet works here, but a combo works best) adds a little kick, while the sour cream keeps the heat in check for a well-rounded dish. It's especially good served over egg noodles, and a little scoop of sauerkraut on top wouldn't be bad either. **SERVES 6 TO 8**

2 tablespoons butter

I small onion, chopped

I red bell pepper, chopped

4 garlic cloves, sliced

3 tablespoons smoked or sweet paprika (or a combination)

I (14.5-ounce) can crushed tomatoes, with juice

½ cup chicken broth

3 pounds skinless, bone-in chicken thighs

Salt and pepper

¼ cup sour cream

Cooked egg noodles, for serving (optional)

TURN on the Sauté function. Once hot, add the butter and let melt. Add the onion and sauté for 2 minutes. Add the bell pepper and garlic and sauté for 1 minute. Add the paprika and cook, stirring, for 1 minute more. Turn off the Sauté function.

ADD the tomatoes and broth and stir. Nestle the chicken thighs into the mixture and season everything with salt and pepper. Secure the lid.

COOK at high pressure for 12 minutes and use a natural release.

REMOVE the chicken with tongs and carefully shred the chicken meat off the bones. Save the bones for broth. Add the meat back to the pot and add the sour cream. Stir and taste for seasoning.

SERVE over egg noodles (if using).

Turkey Black Bean Chili

Turkey Black Bean Chili is a real crowd pleaser. It's hearty with lots of spice without being too spicy, and is excellent topped with a little mound of shredded cheese or sour cream, but needs little else. It'll even please you, the cook, because it's super easy and makes only one dirty dish.

SERVES 4

1 tablespoon canola or grapeseed oil

1½ pounds ground turkey

1 onion, diced

1 red bell pepper, diced

1 jalapeño, seeded and finely diced

4 garlic cloves, minced

2 tablespoons chili powder

2 teaspoons ground cumin

1 teaspoon dried oregano

Salt and pepper

1 (14.5-ounce) can diced tomatoes, with juice

½ cup chicken broth or water

2 (15-ounce) cans black beans, rinsed and drained

1 cup frozen or fresh corn kernels

1 lime, juiced

Shredded cheese or sour cream, for serving

TURN on the Sauté function. Once hot, add the oil followed by the turkey. Break into pieces and sauté until cooked through. Add the onion, bell pepper, jalapeño, and garlic and stir. Add the chili powder, cumin, and oregano, and season with salt and pepper. Stir. Add the tomatoes and broth and turn off the Sauté function. Secure the lid.

COOK at high pressure for 10 minutes and use a natural release.

ADD the beans and corn and turn on the Sauté function. Once simmering, cook for 5 minutes with the lid off. Turn off the Sauté function. Add the lime juice and taste for seasoning.

SERVE topped with cheese or sour cream.

Green Tortilla Soup

Green Tortilla Soup is a multitasker: the chicken breasts roast in the oven while the rest cooks in the pressure cooker. And even more multitasking: corn tortillas are used as a thickener for the soup and as a crispy garnish at the end. You can leave out the jalapeño for a milder dish, or include the seeds for more heat. The hue and much of the flavor comes from salsa verde, a green salsa made with tomatillos that is totally delicious.

SERVES 4

12 ounces boneless, skinless chicken breasts

2 tablespoons olive oil

Salt and pepper

1 small onion, diced

2 celery ribs, diced

1 small green bell pepper, diced

1 small jalapeno, minced

3 garlic cloves, minced

1 teaspoon ground cumin

½ teaspoon chili powder

½ teaspoon dried oregano

3 cups chicken broth

1 (12-ounce) jar salsa verde

1 (15.5-ounce) can pinto beans, rinsed and drained

8 (6-inch) corn tortillas, cut in half and then cut into ½-inch strips

2 cups chopped and packed baby spinach

OPTIONAL TOPPINGS:

Sour cream

Sliced scallions

Fresh cilantro

PREHEAT your oven to 400 degrees.

COAT the chicken breasts in 2 teaspoons oil and season with salt and pepper. Place on a baking sheet with sides and roast for 20 to 25 minutes, depending on the size of the breasts, until cooked through. Let cool.

MEANWHILE, turn on the Sauté function. Once hot, add 1 teaspoon oil followed by the onion, celery, bell pepper, jalapeño, and garlic. Sauté for 3 minutes. Add the cumin, chili powder, and oregano. Stir and cook for 1 minute. Turn off the Sauté function.

ADD the broth, salsa verde, beans, and half of the tortilla strips. Season with salt and pepper and stir. Secure the lid.

COOK at high pressure for 25 minutes and use a natural release.

ONCE the chicken is cool enough to handle, cut into small cubes or shred.

TURN the oven up to 425 degrees. Toss the remaining tortilla strips in 1 tablespoon

(continued)

oil and sprinkle with salt. Spread out into a single layer on a baking sheet and bake for about 5 minutes, until crispy. Keep an eye on them—they burn quickly.

ONCE the pressure has released, add the cooked chicken and spinach to the soup and stir. Replace the lid and let sit for 5 to 10 minutes. Taste for seasoning and serve topped with tortilla strips, sour cream, scallions, and cilantro (if using).

P.S. The chicken can be cooked up to a day ahead of time if you're not the best multitasker.

Preserved Lemon and Garlic Lamb Stew

Preserved lemons are frequently used in Mediterranean and some Middle Eastern cuisines, and you should be using them in your everyday life. The simple ingredient offers a complex punch of citrus and salt, and can be purchased in specialty markets. Preserved lemon goes amazingly well with lamb and a heap of garlic along with fresh veggies. Lamb neck pieces are one of the cheaper cuts of lamb, and they turn fall-apart-tender after a little time in the pressure cooker.

SERVES 4 OR 5

1 tablespoon canola or grapeseed oil

2 pounds bone-in lamb neck pieces

Salt and pepper

1 small onion, sliced

4 garlic cloves, smashed, and 4 garlic cloves, minced

1 cup chicken broth

1 bay leaf

1 (1-pound) turnip, peeled and cut into 1-inch chunks

2 carrots, cut into 1-inch chunks

1 fennel bulb, cut into 1-inch slices

1 small preserved lemon, finely chopped

3 tablespoons finely chopped fresh parsley

TURN on the Sauté function. Once hot, add the oil. Season the lamb pieces with salt and pepper on both sides. Add the lamb in a single layer to the pot and cook, without moving, for 3 minutes. Turn and cook for 3 more minutes. Remove and set aside.

ADD the onion to the pot and sauté for 3 minutes. Add the smashed garlic and stir. Turn off the Sauté function. Add the broth and bay leaf and scrape the bottom of the pot. Add the browned lamb and nestle it into the onion. Secure the lid.

COOK at high pressure for 30 minutes and use a quick release.

ADD the turnip, carrots, and fennel and push down so that they are mostly submerged. Secure the lid.

COOK at high pressure for 4 more minutes and use a natural release.

REMOVE the bay leaf. Pull the meat off the bones and return to the pot (or leave the meat on the bones if desired). Add the preserved lemon and the minced garlic. Turn on the Sauté function and simmer for 3 minutes. Turn off the Sauté function. Let cool for at least 5 minutes, then top with the parsley and serve.

P.S. Preserved lemons are super easy to make if you're thinking ahead. Simply slice a lemon almost all the way through both ways and pack the cuts with salt. Smoosh as many salted lemons as you can in a jar, adding salt between layers, and seal. Store in a cool place and shake every day or so for 3 to 4 weeks, until the peels are tender.

Chicken and Split Pea Soup

Simply put, a good split pea soup is super simple and simply delicious. The classic dish cooks up much faster in the pressure cooker, and a little pancetta and shredded chicken add extra oomph. The soup will thicken up as it cools, so when reheating you may want to add a bit of extra broth.

SERVES 6

2 teaspoons olive oil

2 ounces finely chopped pancetta

1 onion, diced

1 large carrot, diced

4 garlic cloves, minced

1 pound dried split peas, rinsed and drained

6 cups chicken broth

Salt and pepper

2 cups shredded cooked chicken

3 tablespoons chopped fresh parsley

TURN on the Sauté function. Once hot, add the oil followed by the pancetta. Sauté for 2 to 3 minutes, until starting to crisp up. Add the onion and carrot and sauté for 2 more minutes. Add the garlic and stir. Turn off the Sauté function. Add the split peas and broth and season with salt and pepper. Secure the lid.

COOK at high pressure for 20 minutes and use a natural release.

STIR and taste for seasoning. Add the chicken and serve garnished with parsley.

Creamy Spinach and Potato Soup

Potato soup is tasty, but it's not winning any beauty contests. Spinach adds a big punch of green color and some needed nutrition without taking away the creaminess. Gruyère cheese lends a sophisticated, cheesy taste, and I wouldn't blame you if you added some crispy bacon on top too.

SERVES 6

1 tablespoon olive oil

1 small onion, diced

6 garlic cloves, smashed

2 pounds Yukon Gold or white potatoes, peeled and cut into 1-inch chunks

3 cups vegetable or chicken broth

1 (12-ounce) bag frozen spinach, thawed, squeezed of excess moisture, and chopped

1 cup whole milk

Salt and pepper

1 cup shredded Gruyère cheese

2 tablespoons finely chopped fresh parsley

TURN on the Sauté function. Once hot, add the oil followed by the onion. Sauté for 2 minutes. Add the garlic and sauté for 1 minute. Turn off the Sauté function. Add the potatoes and broth. Secure the lid.

COOK at high pressure for 8 minutes and use a quick release.

TURN on the Sauté function to low. Add the spinach and milk and stir. Simmer for 5 minutes, stirring occasionally, and turn off the Sauté function. Season with salt and pepper.

USE an immersion blender to puree the soup, or puree in batches in a blender with the lid cracked. Return to the pot and turn on the Sauté function to low if the soup is no longer hot. Once hot, add the Gruyère and parsley and stir until the cheese is melted. Serve.

Vegetarian Gumbo

A celebrated New Orleans dish, gumbo is a dark, thick stew with lots of flavor. It often includes sausage and shrimp, but this version still satisfies with fragrant spices and hearty beans. Sliced okra adds texture as it helps thicken up the dish. Serve over rice or another grain with hot sauce on the side. SERVES 4 OR 5

2 tablespoons canola or grapeseed oil

2 tablespoons butter

1 large onion, diced

1 red bell pepper, diced

1 green bell pepper, diced

3 celery ribs, diced

4 to 5 large Swiss chard leaves, stems removed and diced and leaves separated and chopped

6 garlic cloves, minced

¼ cup all-purpose flour

2 tablespoons tomato paste

1 teaspoon smoked paprika

¼ teaspoon cayenne pepper, or more to taste

Salt and pepper

2½ cups vegetable broth

1 (15-ounce) can red kidney beans, rinsed and drained

12 ounces fresh okra, sliced

Cooked rice, for serving (optional)

TURN on the Sauté function. Once hot, add the oil and butter. Once the butter has melted, add the onion, bell peppers, celery, and Swiss chard stems. Sauté for 3 minutes, or until the onion begins to turn translucent.

ADD the garlic, flour, tomato paste, paprika, and cayenne. Season with salt and pepper. Cook for 5 minutes, scraping the bottom, until the flour mix is browned. It's okay if some of the flour sticks to the bottom of the pot. Add the broth and thoroughly scrape the bottom of the pot. Turn off the Sauté function. Add the beans. Secure the lid.

COOK at high pressure for 15 minutes and use a natural release.

ONCE the pressure has released, turn on the Sauté function. Add the Swiss chard leaves and okra and cook, uncovered, for 5 minutes, or until thickened. Turn off the Sauté function. Taste for seasoning.

SERVE over rice (if using).

Cheater Ramen
(Japanese Chicken Noodle Soup)

Ramen is one of the best dishes ever conceived, and I am not going to pretend that my version is authentic or anywhere near as complex as what you might find in Japan (just watch the film **Tampopo***). However, it's incredibly tasty and stress-free. Lots of aromatics go into the pressure cooker with chicken wings and bones to make the lightly sweet, salty, and gingery broth. It's ladled over noodles, mushrooms, and chicken for comfort in a bowl.* SERVES 4

1 tablespoon canola or grapeseed oil

1 small onion, quartered

1 large leek, dark greens removed and the rest cut into 1-inch chunks

1 (2-inch) piece of fresh ginger, sliced

1 small bunch scallions, whites cut into 2-inch pieces and greens thinly sliced for garnish

6 garlic cloves, smashed

8 ounces shiitake or cremini mushrooms, 4 ounces halved and 4 ounces thinly sliced

2 skin-on chicken wings and ½ to 1 cup chicken bones (or 4 whole chicken wings)

3 cups chicken broth

3 cups water

3 tablespoons soy sauce

Salt and pepper

4 servings uncooked ramen noodles

2 cups shredded cooked chicken

1 teaspoon sesame oil

2 large soft-boiled eggs, peeled and halved (optional)

TURN on the Sauté function to high. Once hot, add the oil followed by the onion. Cook, without moving, for 2 minutes. Add the leek and ginger and cook for 1 minute more. Add the white pieces of scallion and the garlic and stir. Turn off the Sauté function.

ADD the halved mushrooms, chicken wings and bones, broth, and water. Stir and scrape the bottom. Secure the lid.

COOK at high pressure for 1 hour and use a natural release.

STRAIN the broth through a fine-mesh strainer. Discard the solids. Return the broth to the pot, add the soy sauce, and generously season with salt and pepper. Taste for seasoning.

SET out four soup bowls. Turn on the Sauté function and immediately add the sliced

(continued)

mushrooms. Close the lid and let cook for 3 minutes. Turn off the Sauté function. Using a slotted spoon, remove the mushrooms and add some to each bowl.

MEANWHILE, boil a large pot of water and cook the ramen according to package directions. Drain and add to each bowl. Add ½ cup chicken, a handful of sliced scallions, and a drizzle of sesame oil to each bowl. Top each with broth and ½ soft-boiled egg (if using) and serve.

P.S. Cook bone-in chicken beforehand and use the bones for the broth and the meat for the soup.

Beer and Bean Chili

A quick vegetarian chili chock-full of beans and layers of flavor, Beer and Bean Chili is a classic. A Mexican-style lager imparts the best flavor, but really any standard lager or pilsner will do. Top with cheese and serve with chips, or use it to top hot dogs or nachos. SERVES 4

I tablespoon canola or grapeseed oil	I (12-ounce) bottle or can of lager or pilsner beer
I onion, diced	I (14.5-ounce) can crushed tomatoes
½ green bell pepper, diced	I (15-ounce) can pinto beans, rinsed and drained
½ red bell pepper, diced	
5 garlic cloves, minced	I (15-ounce) can black beans, rinsed and drained
I jalapeño, finely diced	
I tablespoon tomato paste	I (15-ounce) can kidney beans, rinsed and drained
2 tablespoons chili powder	
2 teaspoons ground cumin	Salt and pepper
I teaspoon dried oregano	Shredded cheese or sour cream, for serving (optional)

TURN on the Sauté function. Once hot, add the oil followed by the onion. Sauté for 2 minutes and add the bell peppers and garlic. Sauté for 2 more minutes. Add the jalapeño, tomato paste, chili powder, cumin, and oregano and stir. Cook for 1 minute.

ADD the beer and simmer for 10 minutes, or until reduced by almost half. Turn off the Sauté function. Add the tomatoes and all the beans. Season with salt and pepper. Secure the lid.

COOK at high pressure for 10 minutes and use a natural release.

TASTE for seasoning. Serve topped with cheese or sour cream (if using).

Curried Cauliflower and Butternut Squash Soup

Don't be fooled by the simplicity of Curried Cauliflower and Butternut Squash Soup—it has flavor in spades. Curry paste and curry powder team up with ginger and chile to add layers of flavor, and the creamy veggies add, ya know, creaminess. Serve alongside a salad as a main course, or as a big opener before a noodle or rice dish. SERVES 5 OR 6

1 tablespoon olive oil

1 onion, diced

3 garlic cloves, smashed

1 tablespoon red or yellow curry paste

2 teaspoons curry powder

3½ cups vegetable or chicken broth

1½ pounds butternut squash, peeled and cut into 1-inch chunks

1 head cauliflower, cut into florets (1 to 1½ pounds)

Salt and pepper

1 tablespoon honey

½ lime, juiced

Fresh cilantro, for garnish (optional)

TURN on the Sauté function. Once hot, add the oil followed by the onion and sauté for 3 minutes. Add the garlic and sauté for 1 minute. Add the curry paste and curry powder and stir well. Turn off the Sauté function.

ADD the broth and scrape the bottom of the pot. Add the squash and cauliflower and season with salt and pepper. Push the veggies down so that they are mostly submerged. Secure the lid.

COOK at high pressure for 10 minutes and use a natural release.

ADD the honey and lime juice. Use an immersion blender to blend the soup, or let cool for a bit before pureeing in a blender with the lid cracked. Taste for seasoning.

SERVE topped with cilantro (if using).

Spicy Chicken Sausage Pasta e Fagioli

Spicy Chicken Sausage Pasta e Fagioli is my spin on Martha Rose Shulman's top-notch **New York Times** *recipe that utilizes cooking liquid from the pinto beans to add richness and depth to the soup. Pasta e fagioli translates (as you have probably figured out) to pasta and beans, but it's more than just a stick-to-your-ribs soup. Spicy sausage, tomatoes, and fresh spinach add tons of flavor.*

SERVES 6

I tablespoon plus I teaspoon olive oil

6 ounces fully cooked spicy chicken sausage, sliced into ¼-inch rounds

I onion, diced

4 garlic cloves, minced

I teaspoon chopped fresh rosemary

8 ounces dried pinto beans, presoaked and drained (see page 9)

I bay leaf

6 cups chicken or vegetable broth (or half broth and half water)

Salt and pepper

I (28-ounce) can diced tomatoes with liquid

I cup (6 ounces) dried elbow macaroni

2 cups tightly packed baby spinach

Grated parmesan cheese, for serving

TURN on the Sauté function. Once hot, add 1 tablespoon oil followed by the sausage. Sauté for 3 minutes, or until lightly browned. Remove the sausage and set aside.

ADD 1 teaspoon oil, the onion, garlic, and rosemary and sauté for 2 minutes, scraping the bottom of the pot. Turn off the Sauté function. Add the presoaked beans, the bay leaf, and broth. Season with salt and pepper. Secure the lid.

COOK at high pressure for 10 minutes and use a natural release for 10 minutes followed by a quick release.

TASTE the beans for doneness. Beans should be firm and creamy, not crunchy. If not tender enough, return to pressure for 3 more minutes. Remove the bay leaf.

ADD the tomatoes and turn on the Sauté function. Set the lid loosely on top but do not lock. Once boiling, add the macaroni and cook for 7 minutes with the top off or until al dente. Turn off the Sauté function.

ADD the sausage and spinach and stir until the spinach is wilted. Season as needed and serve topped with parmesan.

P.S. Leave out the chicken sausage and add I teaspoon red pepper flakes for a vegetarian version.

Sauces and Sweet Stuff

Carrot, Ginger, and Turmeric Dressing

Charred Tomato and Pepper Marinara

Many Pepper Hot Sauce

Quince Chutney

Vanilla Stewed Stone Fruit

Mango and Black Sesame Rice Pudding

Salted Caramel Flan

Sweet and Spicy Persimmons

Pineapple-Rum Mug Cakes

Strawberry-Rhubarb Compote

Apple and Pear Sauce

Chai Tea

Hot Spiced Cranberry Cider

Carrot, Ginger, and Turmeric Dressing

I've always loved the bright orange dressing they give you at many Japanese restaurants when you order a sushi box and salad. It's possible to make the gingery dressing without any cooking at all, but you need a really great blender and I don't have one of those. If you've got a crappy blender like mine that needs all the help it can get, this method works really well.

MAKES ABOUT 1 1/2 CUPS; SERVES 6

2 large carrots, cut into 1-inch pieces

1 garlic clove, smashed

1 cup water

1 (1-inch) piece of fresh ginger, peeled and diced

1/4 cup olive oil

4 teaspoons rice wine vinegar

1/2 lemon, juiced

1 teaspoon sesame oil

1 teaspoon honey

1/2 teaspoon ground turmeric

Salt and pepper

ADD the carrots, garlic, and water to your Instant Pot. Secure the lid.

COOK at high pressure for 1 minute and use a quick release.

DRAIN the carrots and garlic, reserving the cooking liquid, and let cool. Once cool, add the carrots and garlic, ginger, olive oil, vinegar, lemon juice, sesame oil, honey, and turmeric to your blender and season with salt and pepper. Add 1/4 cup of the cooking liquid to start.

PUREE until smooth, adding up to 1/2 cup more cooking liquid as needed. The dressing should be thick but pourable. Taste for seasoning.

CHILL in the refrigerator before using. Serve over salad.

Charred Tomato and Pepper Marinara

For a marinara with a little extra somethin' somethin', add red pepper and a little charring from the oven. Broiling does double duty—it adds flavor and makes peeling the veggies a snap. Double this recipe if you're serving a crowd or want to freeze some for later.

MAKES I QUART; SERVES 4 OR 5

I large red bell pepper, stemmed, seeded, and cut into four long strips

2 tablespoons olive oil

Salt and pepper

2 pounds fresh roma tomatoes, halved and most of the seeds removed

I small onion, diced

4 garlic cloves, smashed

I bay leaf

½ teaspoon sugar

PREHEAT your broiler on high and position the rack in the closest position.

TOSS the bell pepper with 2 teaspoons oil and season with salt and pepper. Spread on a baking sheet. Broil, skin side up, for about 5 minutes, or until well charred. Turn and broil for about 3 minutes more, until just lightly charred on the other side. Remove and tent with aluminum foil.

TOSS the tomatoes in 2 teaspoons oil and season with salt and pepper. Broil, cut side up, for 5 to 10 minutes, or until lightly browned on top and juicy. Remove and tent with aluminum foil.

LET the pepper and tomatoes rest until cool enough to handle. Peel the pepper and dice. Peel the tomatoes, reserving any liquid. Discard the peels.

TURN on the Sauté function. Once hot, add 2 teaspoons oil followed by the onion. Cook for about 3 minutes, until translucent and starting to brown. Add the garlic and sauté for 1 more minute. Turn off the Sauté function. Add the diced pepper, tomatoes and juice, and the bay leaf. Secure the lid.

COOK at high pressure for 20 minutes and use a natural release.

REMOVE the bay leaf. Add the sugar and season with salt and pepper. Mash well or puree until the desired consistency is reached. Serve with pasta, in lasagna, or as a dipping sauce.

Many Pepper Hot Sauce

Many Pepper Hot Sauce will have you feelin' hot hot hot, but it's super chill to make. A mix of peppers gives you a wide range of heat and a nice flavor—I like to use 2 ounces serrano, 1 ounce of habanero, and 1 ounce of jalapeño. Whatever peppers you use, be sure to wear gloves the entire time you're making this, including cleanup, and crack all your kitchen windows.

MAKES ABOUT 1 1/2 CUPS

2 carrots, cut into 1-inch pieces

2 garlic cloves, smashed

2 cups plus up to 3 tablespoons water

4 ounces mixed fresh serrano, habanero, jalapeño, and Fresno peppers, stemmed and chopped

⅓ cup fresh lime juice

2 tablespoons white vinegar

½ teaspoon table salt

ADD the carrots, garlic, and 2 cups water to your Instant Pot. Secure the lid.

COOK at high pressure for 3 minutes and use a natural release.

DRAIN the carrots and garlic and let cool a bit. Add the peppers, lime juice, vinegar, salt, and cooked carrots and garlic to your blender. Blend until completely pureed, adding up to 3 tablespoons water as needed to make a thinner sauce.

PUSH the sauce through a fine-mesh strainer (optional) and into a jar and let sit in the refrigerator for a couple of days before using. Store in the refrigerator and use within 2 months.

P.S. Double or triple this recipe if you'd like to give some as gifts. It looks pretty in small glass jars.

Quince Chutney

Quince is a rock-hard fall fruit that looks kind of like a big blobby yellow pear and smells intoxicating. Quince Chutney is one great way to use the fruit—it's tangy, sweet, and savory, and excellent served with a spicy curry or even roasted or grilled meats. To prepare the quince, wash and scrub off all of the fuzz. Peel with a vegetable peeler and quarter with a sharp knife. Remove the core and seeds and dice the remaining fruit. Be careful, it's tough fruit and can be hard to cut.

MAKES ABOUT 3 CUPS

1 tablespoon canola or grapeseed oil

1 shallot, minced

1 serrano pepper, whole

1 tablespoon grated or finely minced fresh ginger

½ teaspoon ground cinnamon

½ teaspoon ground cardamom, or 2 green cardamom pods

1 cup brown sugar

1 cup water

1½ pounds fresh quinces, peeled, cored, and diced

1 Granny Smith apple, peeled, cored, and diced

½ cup dried sweet cherries, cranberries, or currants

Salt and pepper

½ cup apple cider vinegar

½ lemon, juiced

TURN on the Sauté function. Once hot, add the oil followed by the shallot and serrano pepper. Sauté for 1 minute. Add the ginger, cinnamon, and cardamom and stir. Turn off the Sauté function.

ADD the brown sugar and water and stir. Add the quinces, apple, and dried fruit and season with salt and pepper. Secure the lid.

COOK at high pressure for 20 minutes and use a natural release for 10 minutes followed by a quick release.

THE quince should be tender but not mushy. Remove the serrano pepper and cardamom pods (if using) and drain off most of the liquid. Return to the pot and add the vinegar and lemon juice.

TASTE for seasoning and cool overnight in the refrigerator. Store in the refrigerator for up to 2 weeks.

Vanilla Stewed Stone Fruit

Vanilla Stewed Stone Fruit with Greek yogurt is one of my favorite things to eat for breakfast. The nectarines, plums, and apricots are tender with intense fruity flavor, while real vanilla and brown sugar add fragrant sweetness. Serve warm or chilled with yogurt or, for a real treat, vanilla ice cream.   SERVES 3 OR 4

1½ pounds firm-ripe nectarines, plums, or apricots (a combination is best), cut in half and pitted

¼ cup brown sugar

1 vanilla bean pod

3 green cardamom pods (optional)

½ cup water

ADD the fruit to your Instant Pot in as close to a single layer as possible. Sprinkle the brown sugar over top. Cut the vanilla bean pod in half lengthwise and scrape out the seeds. Add both the seeds and the pod to the pot. Add the cardamom (if using) and the water. Secure the lid.

COOK at high pressure for 4 minutes and use a natural release.

REMOVE the fruit with a slotted spoon and set aside. Turn on the Sauté function. Let the liquid cook for about 10 minutes, until it is reduced by at least two-thirds and syrupy. Remove the vanilla bean and cardamom pods (if using). Turn off the Sauté function and let cool for 5 minutes.

SERVE the fruit topped with the syrup.

P.S. I don't use peaches so that I don't have to peel any fruit (I'm lazy). If you don't mind peeling or don't mind peach fuzz, then feel free to include some.

Mango and Black Sesame Rice Pudding

The Instant Pot is the perfect vessel for rice pudding, gently cooking the rice and milk until creamy without the risk of burning. Eggs are carefully added at the end, making the pudding thicker and more luxurious. Black sesame paste, an Asian treat, adds sweet nuttiness. If you can't find it at a supermarket near you, make your own. Grind up 1 heaping tablespoon black sesame seeds using a spice grinder or small food processor. Once well-ground and paste-like, combine with 1 tablespoon honey.

SERVES 6

1 cup short-grain white rice, well rinsed and drained	2 large eggs, beaten, at room temperature
5 cups whole milk	1 tablespoon black sesame paste
⅔ cup sugar	1 teaspoon vanilla extract
1 pinch salt	1 large ripe mango, peeled and diced

COMBINE the rice, milk, sugar, and salt in your Instant Pot. Whisk together and secure the lid.

COOK at high pressure for 10 minutes and use a natural release.

WHISK the cooked rice and milk mixture well. Temper the eggs by slowly adding 1 cup of the hot milky rice to the eggs while whisking constantly. Add that mixture to the Instant Pot slowly, whisking the whole time.

TURN on the Sauté function. Whisk until the mixture is simmering and starting to thicken up. Turn off the Sauté function.

ADD the black sesame paste and vanilla and mix well.

ALLOW the rice pudding to cool. It will thicken greatly as it sits. Serve warm or cold topped with fresh mango.

Salted Caramel Flan

This wonderfully eggy, silky smooth flan is based on my fellow pressure cooker maven Sara Bir's recipe. The salty caramel sets off the subtle and sweet custard perfectly, and it looks lovely on a plate. Note that if you're using an 8-inch pan, triple-check that it'll fit in your cooker, and leave the handles on the trivet down so that the flan can squeeze in. SERVES 8

1¾ cups water

¾ cup sugar

¾ teaspoon sea salt or kosher salt

2 large eggs

4 large egg yolks

1 (14-ounce) can sweetened condensed milk

2 cups whole milk

1 teaspoon vanilla extract

¼ teaspoon table salt

PREPARE a 7- or 8-inch metal cake pan or ceramic baking dish that will fit inside your Instant Pot. Fold a 1½-foot-long piece of aluminum foil to make a long, 2-inch-wide sling. Position the middle of the sling under the pan so that the ends stick up on either side, creating makeshift handles.

ADD the trivet to your Instant Pot and add 1½ cups water, or just enough to reach the underside of the trivet.

COMBINE the sugar and ¼ cup water in a medium saucepan. Cook over medium heat, stirring until the sugar dissolves. Stop stirring, turn the heat up to medium-high, and bring the mixture to a boil. Cook, swirling the pan occasionally (but not stirring), until the mixture turns a deep amber color, 6 to 10 minutes. Quickly add the sea salt and swirl to combine. Immediately pour into the baking dish before the caramel solidifies. Let cool for at least 5 minutes.

IN a mixing bowl, whisk the eggs and egg yolks. Add the sweetened condensed milk, whole milk, vanilla, and table salt. Whisk until the mixture is totally combined. Pour into the baking pan on top of the caramel. Cover tightly with aluminum foil. Place the pan with the foil sling on the trivet, making sure that the sling isn't getting in the way of the lid. Secure the lid.

COOK at high pressure for 40 minutes and use a natural release.

CAREFULLY remove the pan using the foil sling. Remove the foil on top and set on a wire rack. Let cool to room temperature before refrigerating, uncovered, overnight.

TO SERVE, run a paring knife around the very outside of the flan. Invert onto a serving platter.

P.S. Remember that there's caramel in there! Use a serving dish that can hold the caramel sauce, too.

Sweet and Spicy Persimmons

Persimmons are a highlight of the winter fruit season, and a real treat if you know what to do with them. Fuyu persimmons (the most common variety in the United States) look like a cartoon tomato, and are fully orange and plump once ripe. To make them sweet and spicy, cook them in your Instant Pot with a simple mulled wine and sugar. The fruit will emerge fragrant without turning to mush, making it the ultimate wintertime treat.   SERVES 4

½ cup red wine

¼ cup sugar

1 (1-inch) piece of fresh ginger, sliced

1 cinnamon stick

4 whole cloves

½ cup fresh orange juice

4 firm-ripe Fuyu persimmons, stemmed and peeled and cut into 8 wedges, seeds removed

TURN on the Sauté function. Add the wine, sugar, ginger, cinnamon stick, and cloves. Bring to a simmer and cook for 1 minute. Turn off the Sauté function.

ADD the orange juice. Add the persimmon slices in a single layer, cut side down. Secure the lid.

COOK at high pressure for 3 minutes and use a natural release.

TURN the slices over and let sit in the wine and juice for 5 minutes. Serve drizzled with the cooking liquid.

Pineapple-Rum Mug Cakes

Mug cakes are all the rage in microwave cooking, and they're great as a single-serving dessert. I'm into the idea of eating warm cake any time I want, but I'm a weirdo who doesn't own a microwave. It takes a few more minutes to make a mug cake in the pressure cooker, but it's just as easy and you can make two at once. The pineapple-rum version is dense and moist, and especially good with fresh whipped cream on top. Halve the recipe for a single serving.

SERVES 2

Cooking spray

1 cup water

3 tablespoons unsalted butter, melted

2 tablespoons granulated sugar

1 tablespoon plus 1 teaspoon packed brown sugar

2 teaspoons dark rum

½ teaspoon vanilla extract

½ cup all-purpose flour

1 teaspoon baking powder

1 pinch salt

¼ cup whole milk

4 tablespoons crushed or finely chopped pineapple, drained and squeezed of excess liquid

Fresh whipped cream or vanilla ice cream (optional)

PREPARE two heatproof, standard-sized coffee mugs or ramekins by spraying the inside with cooking spray. Add the trivet and water to your Instant Pot.

IN a small mixing bowl, combine the melted butter, granulated sugar, and brown sugar and mix using a small whisk or fork. Add 1 teaspoon rum and the vanilla and mix well. Add the flour, baking powder, and salt and mix into a paste. Add the milk and mix just until well combined. Fold in 2 tablespoons pineapple.

DIVIDE the batter evenly between the two mugs. Set the mugs on the trivet, avoiding the sides of the pot. Secure the lid.

COOK at high pressure for 18 minutes and use a quick release.

MEANWHILE, combine 2 tablespoons pineapple and 1 teaspoon rum and stir. Let sit.

REMOVE the lid, careful not to drip any condensation onto the cakes. Test a cake with a toothpick—if it comes out clean or with a couple of crumbs attached, the cakes are done. If the toothpick is wet, return to pressure for 2 minutes.

CAREFULLY remove the mugs (don't burn yourself) and let cool for a few minutes.

SERVE topped with whipped cream or ice cream (if using) and the rum pineapple.

Strawberry-Rhubarb Compote

Straddling the line between fresh fruit and jam, compote combines barely cooked fruit and sugar syrup for a wonderfully fruity topping. Rhubarb cooks down to make a sweet-tart sauce, and fresh strawberries retain much of their texture and fresh flavor. Adjust the sugar according to how sweet your berries are, and serve the compote with plain Greek yogurt for breakfast or over ice cream for dessert.   MAKES 1 QUART; SERVES 6 TO 8

¾ to 1 cup sugar

½ cup water

1 pound rhubarb, trimmed and chopped

1 pint strawberries, hulled and quartered

1 teaspoon fresh lemon juice

¼ teaspoon vanilla extract

TURN on the Sauté function. Add the sugar and water and cook for 2 to 3 minutes, until most of the sugar is dissolved. Turn off the Sauté function and add the rhubarb. Secure the lid.

COOK at high pressure for 3 minutes and use a natural release.

ADD the strawberries, lemon juice, and vanilla and stir. Taste and add more sugar if needed. Let cool, then refrigerate until chilled and serve cold.

Apple and Pear Sauce

Ordinary applesauce is elevated with ripe pears, a touch of butter, and brown sugar, turning it into something worth serving over ice cream or pound cake. It's delectable on its own too, served warm or cold. If you have a food mill, then congratulations! This recipe just got a whole lot easier. Don't bother peeling or coring, just quarter the fruit, cook it, and run it through the food mill before adding the sugar and seasoning. MAKES 5 CUPS; SERVES 6 TO 8

2 tablespoons unsalted butter

3 pounds apples (a mixture of varieties), peeled, cored, and quartered

2 pounds pears, such Bosc, peeled, cored, and quartered

1 orange, juiced (about ⅓ cup)

2 tablespoons brown sugar

½ teaspoon ground cinnamon

½ teaspoon vanilla extract

TURN on the Sauté function. Once hot, add the butter and let melt. Add the apples and pears and turn off the Sauté function. Add the orange juice. Secure the lid.

COOK at high pressure for 10 minutes and use a natural release for 10 minutes followed by a quick release.

ADD the brown sugar, cinnamon, and vanilla. Mash or puree the sauce to the desired consistency. Serve warm or chilled. Store in the refrigerator for up to 5 days.

Chai Tea

Forget that powdered stuff. Homemade chai tea made from real, whole spices is totally next level. The pressure cooker does a fantastic job of extracting the flavor from the spices without evaporating any of the water. It's delish served hot or cold, and you can use decaf, rooibos, or even green tea instead of black tea.

SERVES 4 OR 5

20 whole cloves

15 green cardamom pods

2 teaspoons black peppercorns

2 large cinnamon sticks

1 (3-inch) piece of fresh ginger, sliced

4 cups water

½ cup honey

5 teaspoons loose black tea such as Darjeeling, or 5 black tea bags

1 to 3 cups milk or nondairy milk (soy, almond, or coconut)

ADD the cloves, cardamom, peppercorns, and cinnamon sticks to your Instant Pot. Crush the spices with the bottom of a jar or other blunt instrument. Add the ginger and water and secure the lid.

COOK at high pressure for 7 minutes and use a natural release for 5 minutes followed by a quick release.

ADD the honey and black tea and stir. Let steep for 4 minutes. Meanwhile, if serving warm, heat the milk in the microwave or on the stovetop until warm.

STRAIN the tea mixture to remove the spices and tea leaves. Add tea to each mug and milk to taste (about ¼ cup milk for a really flavorful brew, or up to ¾ cup for a milder, creamier brew) and serve.

P.S. I highly recommend doubling this recipe, since it will keep in the fridge for up to a week. Let the pressure naturally release for 10 minutes or longer, since you'll have twice as much hot liquid inside.

Hot Spiced Cranberry Cider

Hot spiced cider is so warming on a cold night, and cranberry makes the drink pleasantly tart and extra festive. Add a little brown sugar if it's not sweet enough for you, and garnish with some bright red fresh cranberries for the ultimate holiday drink. SERVES 6 TO 8

6 cups apple cider

4 cups cranberry juice cocktail

3 cinnamon sticks

½ teaspoon whole cloves

1 orange, sliced

2 tablespoons brown sugar (optional)

1 handful fresh cranberries (optional)

ADD the cider, cranberry juice, cinnamon sticks, cloves, and orange to your Instant Pot. Secure the lid.

COOK at high pressure for 8 minutes and use a natural release.

REMOVE the spices by straining or using a slotted spoon. Add brown sugar to taste and serve hot garnished with cranberries (if using).

INDEX

Page numbers in *italics* refer to recipe photographs.

Shakshuka with Harissa and Feta, 23
Spicy Bolognese, 47
Spicy Chicken Sausage Pasta e Fagioli, *150,*
    151
Tamale Pie, *80,* 81
Turkey and Black Bean Chili, 139
Vegetarian Stuffed Cabbage, 74–75
White Bean Ragu Spaghetti, 66
tortilla(s):
    Lazy Al Pastor, 43
    Soup, Green, *140,* 141–42
    Vietnamese Brisket Tacos, 48, *49*
trivet, 5
Turkey and Black Bean Chili, 139
turnips:
    Beef Roast with Leek and, 50–51

Preserved Lemon and Garlic Lamb Stew,
    142–43

V

Vanilla Stewed Stone Fruit, 159

W

Wheat Berry Bowl, Brown Butter and Pear, 26,
    27
wine, 10

Z

zucchini
    Charred Vegetable and Cheese Grits,
        64–66, *65*

LAUREL RANDOLPH has been a food writer for ten years and a cook since she was old enough to properly hold a whisk. She is the bestselling author of *The Instant Pot® Electric Pressure Cooker Cookbook: Easy Recipes for Fast & Healthy Meals*. She has written for numerous publications including *The Spruce*, *Paste Magazine*, *Serious Eats*, and *Table Matters*.